Presidential Elections Handbook

McDougal Littell
A HOUGHTON MIFFLIN COMPANY
Evanston, Illinois • Boston • Dallas

This *Presidential Elections Handbook* may be used separately or as a companion to the following American history textbooks published by McDougal Littell:

Creating America for grades 7 and 8

The Americans for high school students

Credits

Virginia A. Carley, Social Studies Consultant; Skokie, Illinois

Bruce Eddy, Social Studies Teacher; Evanston Township High School, Evanston, Illinois

Nancy Wiles DeGuiseppe, Social Studies Consultant; Des Plaines, Illinois

Thomas Kucharski, Social Studies Teacher; Loyola Academy, Wilmette, Illinois

Leonard P. Miller, Social Studies Consultant; Phoenix, Arizona

Art Credits

Washington through L.B. Johnson, National Archives.

Nixon, Carter, Reagan, Clinton, AP/Wide World Photos.

George H.W. Bush, © Wally McNamee/Corbis.

George W. Bush, Bush-Cheney 2000, Inc.

ISBN-13: 978-0-618-53630-6   ISBN-10: 0-618-53630-2

7 8 9 10 11 - MJT - 12 11 10 09 08

McDougal Littell
Presidential Elections Handbook

Contents

Presidential Facts at a Glance

President	Birth–Death	Vice–President	Party	Term of Office	Popular Vote	Percent	Electoral Vote
George Washington	1732–1799	John Adams	none	1789–1797	unknown unknown		69 132
John Adams	1735–1826	Thomas Jefferson	Federalist	1797–1801	unknown		71
Thomas Jefferson	1743–1826	Aaron Burr George Clinton	Democratic–Republican	1801–1809	unknown unknown		73 162
James Madison	1751–1836	George Clinton Elbridge Gerry	Democratic–Republican	1809–1817	unknown unknown		122 128
James Monroe	1758–1831	Daniel D. Tompkins	Democratic–Republican	1817–1825	unknown unknown		183 231
John Quincy Adams	1767–1848	John C. Calhoun	Democratic–Republican	1825–1829	108,740	30.6%	84
Andrew Jackson	1767–1845	John C. Calhoun Martin Van Buren	Democrat	1829–1837	647,286 687,502	56.0% 56.5%	178 219
Martin Van Buren	1782–1862	Richard M. Johnson	Democrat	1837–1841	765,483	50.9%	170
William H. Harrison	1773–1841	John Tyler	Whig	1841	1,274,624	53.1%	234
John Tyler	1790–1862	*	Whig	1841–1845	Succeeded after Harrison's death		
James K. Polk	1795–1849	George M. Dallas	Democrat	1845–1849	1,338.464	49.6%	170
Zachary Taylor	1784–1850	Millard Fillmore	Whig	1849–1850	1,360,967	47.3%	163
Millard Fillmore	1800–1874	*	Whig	1850–1853	Succeeded after Taylor's death		
Franklin Pierce	1804–1869	William R. King	Democrat	1853–1857	1,601,117	50.9%	254
James Buchanan	1791–1868	John C. Breckinridge	Democrat	1857–1861	1,832,955	45.3%	174
Abraham Lincoln	1809–1865	Hannibal Hamlin Andrew Johnson	Republican	1861–1865	1,865,593 2,206,938	39.8% 55.0%	180 212
Andrew Johnson	1808–1875	*	Democrat	1865–1869	Succeeded after Lincoln's death		
Ulysses S. Grant	1822–1885	Schuyler Colfax Henry Wilson	Republican	1869–1877	3,013,421 3,596,745	52.7% 55.6%	214 286
Rutherford B. Hayes	1822–1893	William A. Wheeler	Republican	1877–1881	4,036,572	48.0%	185
James A. Garfield	1831–1881	Chester A. Arthur	Republican	1881	4,453,295	48.5%	214
Chester A. Arthur	1829–1886	*	Republican	1881–1885	Succeeded after Garfield's death		
Grover Cleveland	1837–1908	Thomas Hendricks	Democrat	1885–1889	4,879,507	48.5%	219
Benjamin Harrison	1833–1901	Levi P. Morton	Republican	1889–1893	5,447,129	47.9%	233

Grover Cleveland	1837–1908	Adlai E. Stevenson	Democrat	1893–1897	5,555,426	46.0%	277
William McKinley	1843–1901	Garret A. Hobart Theodore Roosevelt	Republican	1897–1901	7,102,246 7,218,491	51.0% 51.7%	271 292
Theodore Roosevelt	1858–1919	* Charles Fairbanks	Republican	1901–1909	Succeeded after McKinley's Death 7,628,461	56.4%	33
William Howard Taft	1857–1930	James S. Sherman	Republican	1909–1913	7,675,320	51.6%	321
Woodrow Wilson	1856–1924	Thomas R. Marshall	Democrat	1913–1921	6,296,547 9,127,695	41.9% 49.4%	435 277
Warren G. Harding	1865–1923	Calvin Coolidge	Republican	1921–1923	16,143,407	60.4%	404
Calvin Coolidge	1872–1933	Charles G. Dawes	Republican	1923–1929	15,718,211	54.0%	382
Herbert C. Hoover	1874–1964	Charles Curtis	Republican	1929–1933	21,391,993	58.2%	444
Franklin D. Roosevelt	1882–1945	John Nance Garner Henry A. Wallace Harry S. Truman	Democrat	1933–1945	22,809,638 27,752,869 27,307,819 25,606,585	57.4% 60.8% 54.8% 53.5%	472 523 449 432
Harry S. Truman	1884–1972	* Alben W. Barkley	Democrat	1945–1953	Succeeded after Roosevelt's Death 24,105,812	49.5%	303
Dwight D. Eisenhower	1890–1969	Richard M. Nixon	Republican	1953–1961	33,936,234 35,590,472	55.1% 57.4%	442 457
John F. Kennedy	1917–1963	Lyndon B. Johnson	Democrat	1961–1963	34,227,096	49.5%	303
Lyndon B. Johnson	1908–1973	* Herbert H. Humphrey	Democrat	1963–1969	Succeeded after Kennedy's Death 43,129,484	61.1%	486
Richard M. Nixon	1913–1994	Spiro T. Agnew Gerald R. Ford	Republican	1969–1974	31,785,480 47,169,911	43.4% 60.7%	301 520
Gerald R. Ford	1913–	Nelson A. Rockefeller	Republican	1974–1977	Succeeded after Nixon's resignation		
James E. Carter	1924–	Walter F. Mondale	Democrat	1977–1981	40,825,839	50.0%	297
Ronald W. Reagan	1911–2004	George H.W. Bush	Republican	1981–1989	43,904,153 53,354,037	51.0% 58.0%	489 525
George H.W. Bush	1924–	J. Danforth Quayle	Republican	1989–1993	48,886,097	53.4%	426
William J. Clinton	1946–	Albert Gore, Jr.	Democrat	1993–2001	44,908,223 47,401,054	43.0% 49.2%	370 379
George W. Bush	1946–	Richard B. Cheney	Republican	2001–	50,456,169 62,028,194	47.9% 50.7%	271 286

*No succession for Vice–President until 1967.

Little Known Facts About the Presidents

Official information about American Presidents is commonly available. Many people also enjoy learning about the unusual aspects of the Presidents. Consider the following oddities:

Washington's Birthday
George Washington's birthday is actually February 11th, not the 22nd. The calendar was changed during his lifetime. In 1752 America and Great Britain adopted the Gregorian calendar over the Julian calendar. With that adoption, eleven days were "lost."

Virginia, Home of Presidents
Seven of the first twelve Presidents were from Virginia. They are:

George Washington	William H. Harrison
Thomas Jefferson	John Tyler
James Madison	Zachary Taylor
James Monroe	

Ohio, Another Popular Home
Seven Presidents were born in Ohio. They are:

Ulysses S. Grant	Benjamin Harrison
Rutherford B. Hayes	William McKinley
James A. Garfield	William Taft
Warren G. Harding	

Humble Beginnings
In addition to Abraham Lincoln, the following Presidents were born in log cabins:

James Buchanan	Andrew Jackson
Millard Fillmore	Zachary Taylor
James Garfield	

The 4th of July
Two Presidents died on the fiftieth anniversary of the Declaration of Independence, John Adams and Thomas Jefferson. Both died on July 4, 1826, within hours of each other. They were the only Presidents to have signed the Declaration. Calvin Coolidge, our 30th President, was born on July 4, 1872.

Beware of Zero Years!
Since 1800, seven Presidents elected in zero years have died in office. They were: 1840—William H. Harrison; 1860—Abraham Lincoln; 1880—James Garfield; 1900—William McKinley; 1920—Warren Harding; 1940—Franklin Roosevelt; 1960—John Kennedy.

Good Connections
Franklin Roosevelt claimed to have ancestors who came to Massachusetts on the Mayflower. Genealogists believe he was also related by blood or marriage to eleven Presidents including Washington, John Adams, Madison, John Quincy Adams, Van Buren, William Henry Harrison, Taylor, Grant, Benjamin Harrison, Theodore Roosevelt, and Taft.

Employment History
Only James Madison never had a job other than a politician. Most were lawyers before becoming President. Twenty-four past Presidents were admitted to the bar as attorneys. These included J. Adams, Jefferson, Monroe, J.Q. Adams, Jackson, Van Buren, Tyler, Polk, Fillmore, Pierce, Buchanan, Lincoln, Hayes, Garfield, Arthur, Cleveland, B. Harrison, McKinley, Taft, Wilson, Coolidge, F.D. Roosevelt, Nixon, Ford, and Clinton.

The following were school teachers and educators: John Adams, Fillmore, Garfield, Arthur, McKinley, Harding, Lyndon Johnson, Taft, Wilson, and Eisenhower.

Like Father, Like Son
When George W. Bush was elected President in 2000, he and his father, George Herbert Walker Bush, became only the second father and son pair to have been elected president. The first pair was John Adams and his son John Quincy Adams.

College Degrees
Some presidents attended, but did not graduate, from college: Monroe, William H. Harrison, and McKinley. Some never went to college: Washington, Jackson, Van Buren, Taylor, Fillmore, Lincoln, Andrew Johnson, Cleveland, and Truman.

Cherry Blossom Time
While Taft was Governor of the Philippines, Mrs. Taft visited Tokyo and fell in love with the lovely cherry trees there. As First Lady, Helen Taft was instrumental in arranging the gift of 3,000 Japanese cherry trees, which were planted in Washington, D.C. in 1912.

Deaths in Office
Four Presidents have been assassinated: Lincoln, Garfield, McKinley, and Kennedy. Four other Presidents have died in office: William H. Harrison, Taylor, Harding, and Franklin Roosevelt.

Minority Presidents
It is more common than generally thought that the United States has a President elected without a majority of the popular vote. Minority Presidents include: John Quincy Adams, Polk, Taylor, Buchanan, Lincoln, Hayes, Garfield, Cleveland, Benjamin Harrison, Wilson, Truman, Kennedy, Nixon, Carter, Clinton, and George W. Bush.

Reelection Jinx!
No President whose last name begins with H has been reelected. They are:

William H. Harrison	Rutherford Hayes
Benjamin Harrison	Herbert Hoover
William Harding	

Three Presidents in One Year
In the years 1841 and 1881, the country had three Presidents in one year. On March 3, 1841, Martin Van Buren completed his term in office. William Henry Harrison died a month after his inauguration, and John Tyler became President.

Rutherford B. Hayes ended his term on March 3, 1881 and James Garfield was inaugurated. Garfield died in September and Chester A. Arthur became the President.

Lincoln's "Lost Speech"
While most Americans are familiar with lines from Abraham Lincoln's Gettysburg Address, no one can recall the words to his famous speech of 1856 at the first Republican convention in Illinois. The speech followed the burning of a Kansas town by a group supporting slavery. The audience was so mesmerized by Lincoln's denunciation of the proslavery movement that nobody took notes.

"I'm not in this for the money"
Three Presidents did not accept a salary during their terms in office. Herbert Hoover and John Kennedy refused payment, while Martin Van Buren collected a lump sum at the end of his term.

Electoral College and Map

The Electoral College was created by the United States Constitution. Our present system was adopted in 1804 with the passage of the Twelfth Amendment. The Electoral College is a group having the responsibility of electing the President and Vice-President. Generally, state committees or conventions of each political party select candidates for electors. Most states list only the Presidential and Vice-Presidential candidates and not the electors on the ballot. As a result, many voters do not realize who the electors are, nor do the voters realize that they vote only indirectly for the President and Vice-President. The number of votes each state has in the Electoral College equals the total of its senators and representatives in Congress.

In December following the Presidential election, the electors meet, usually in their state capitals, to vote for President and Vice-President. Their sealed ballots are delivered to the president of the U.S. Senate. In January at a joint session of Congress, the electoral votes are counted. The candidate with a majority of electoral votes is declared the winner and becomes President of the United States. If no candidate has a majority, the members of the House of Representatives choose the President.

The vote in the Electoral College is usually a routine ceremony. Some want to abolish the Electoral College and establish the direct election of the President by popular vote. You might debate this issue in class.

ELECTORAL VOTES

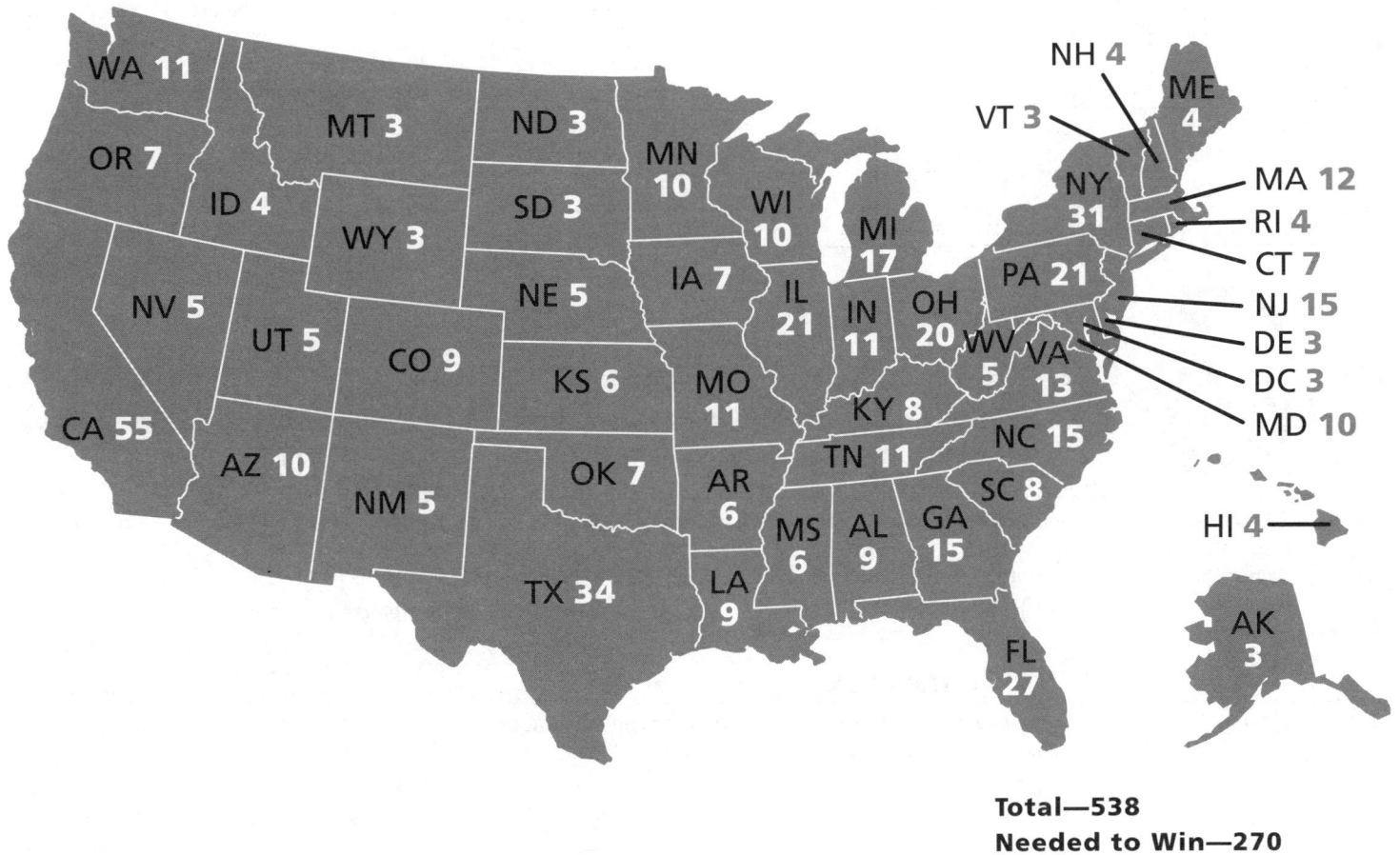

WA 11
OR 7
ID 4
MT 3
WY 3
ND 3
SD 3
MN 10
WI 10
NH 4
VT 3
ME 4
NY 31
MA 12
RI 4
CT 7
NJ 15
DE 3
DC 3
MD 10
NV 5
UT 5
CO 9
NE 5
IA 7
MI 17
IL 21
IN 11
OH 20
PA 21
WV 5
VA 13
CA 55
AZ 10
NM 5
KS 6
MO 11
KY 8
TN 11
NC 15
SC 8
OK 7
AR 6
MS 6
AL 9
GA 15
TX 34
LA 9
FL 27
HI 4
AK 3

Total—538
Needed to Win—270

Washington Leads Nation in 1789

THE CANDIDATES

George Washington was everyone's choice to lead the infant nation. The Electoral College unanimously elected him President.

John Adams, a Harvard-educated patriot, was elected our nation's first Vice-President.

THE CAMPAIGN

1. Washington's legendary reputation at home and abroad made him the only logical candidate for the office of the first President of the United States.
2. Alexander Hamilton, Washington's close friend, had to persuade Washington to delay his retirement. Hamilton appealed to the reluctant candidate's sense of duty by saying, "every public and personal consideration will demand from you an acquiescence in what will certainly be the unanimous wish of your country."

THE ISSUES

	Washington (No Party)	No Opposition
Foreign	For international recognition, peace in the Northwest Territory	.
Economic	Established financial order by paying off foreign debts and funding domestic debts	
Social	For a Bill of Rights	
Personal	Washington's reputation was Impeccable	

QUOTES & CUSTOMS

Titles Nobody knew what to call the President. Congress considered such titles as "His Excellency," "His Serene Highness," and "His High Mightiness" before settling on the simpler "Mr. President."

Precedents Because of Washington:

- Executive officers of newly created departments formed an advisory cabinet.
- Presidents serve no more than two terms.

THE LESSONS

1. The executive department has a tendency to grow. Only two people, Washington and Adams, made up the executive branch when they were elected in 1789. Today, over 2,800,000 work for the executive branch.
2. The transition from a confederation to a republic was achieved peacefully and reasonably without violence and bloodshed.

Washington Wins Unanimously Again in 1792

THE CANDIDATES

George Washington ran unopposed for reelection despite his refusal to announce his candidacy. Once again, Washington was the unanimous choice of the Electoral College.

John Adams, still bitterly disappointed with the office of Vice-President, agreed to stay on and looked forward to better things in the future.

THE CAMPAIGN

1. Political parties began to emerge from the differences of opinion between Alexander Hamilton's supporters (Federalists) and Thomas Jefferson's supporters (Democratic-Republicans).
2. Vigorous public debate was carried on in two newspapers—National Gazette and Gazette of the United States.

THE ISSUES

	Washington (Federalist)	(Republicans)
Foreign	Supported Britain and feared the French Revolution	Favored the French Revolution; against the British monarchy
Economic	For a national bank and a "loose interpretation" of the Constitution	For a "strict interpretation" of the Constitution and no national bank
Social	Represented "the rich, the well-born, and the able"	Represented the small farmers and wage-earners in towns
Personal	Washington did not like political factions	

QUOTES & CUSTOMS

Keep It Brief Washington's second inaugural address was the shortest in history—133 words.

Smile By age fifty-seven, George Washington had lost all his own teeth. During his constant search for comfortable teeth, he had a French dentist make him a set carved from rhinoceros ivory.

Farewell Address "The great rule of conduct for us in regard to foreign nations is in extending our commercial relations [and] to have as little political connection as possible."

Eulogy At Washington's funeral, Light Horse Harry Lee gave this famous description of Washington: "First in war, first in peace and first in the hearts of his countrymen, he was second to none…

THE LESSONS

1. Political party differences would not destroy national unity.
2. Newspapers would encourage public information and debate.

Adams Moves Up in 1796

THE CANDIDATES

John Adams, a two-term Vice-President, was Washington's heir apparent and the logical Federalist candidate. **Thomas Pinckney** successfully negotiated the popular Pinckney Treaty of 1795. The Federalists hoped that this South Carolina candidate would capture the Vice Presidency.

Thomas Jefferson, leader of the Democratic-Republican (Republican) Party, left Washington's cabinet in 1793 after continual disputes with his rival Hamilton. **Aaron Burr,** the senator from New York, was the Democratic-Republican candidate for the Vice-Presidency.

THE CAMPAIGN

1. Neither candidate took an active part in the campaign. They left electioneering to party followers who used handbills, pamphlets, and party newspapers.
2. Party caucuses developed in the form of congressional meetings to choose party candidates.
3. Adams won by three votes and wound up with a Vice-President from an opposing party.

THE ISSUES

	Adams (Federalist)	Jefferson (Republican)
Foreign	Favored Britain and thought harsh and violent reprisals of the French Revolution were extreme	Sympathized with the French Revolution
Economic	For a strong federal economic policy	For decentralized power
Social	Perceived as the party of the aristocracy	Perceived as a party of "the people"
Personal	Accused of starting a hereditary monarchy in the U.S.	Denounced as wanting to overthrow the Constitution

QUOTES & CUSTOMS

Longevity John Adams had the longest life span, nearly ninety-one years, and the longest-lasting marriage, fifty-four years, of any President.

White House The Adams family was the first to live in the then unfinished White House. John Adams's prayer ("I pray to Heaven to bestow the best of blessings on this House and all that hereafter inhabit it…May none but honest and wise men ever rule under this roof.") was later carved on the mantel in the State Dining Room.

President's Choice Adams made the mistake of keeping all of Washington's cabinet—a group more loyal to Hamilton than to Adams.

THE LESSONS

1. Peaceful change of chief executives is possible in a republic.
2. Party caucus meetings could make or break candidates.
3. Geographic balance for party candidates was important to national appeal.

Jefferson Leads a Change of Party in 1800

THE CANDIDATES

Thomas Jefferson, Republican Vice-President, challenged Adams's leadership for a second time. The Vice-Presidential candidate, **Aaron Burr,** Republican politician from New York, was an archenemy of Hamilton and later killed him in a duel in 1804.

John Adams, the incumbent Federalist President, faced torrents of criticism because of his policy on France and the Alien and Sedition Acts. **Charles Cotesworth Pinckney** came from South Carolina and balanced the Federalist ticket.

THE CAMPAIGN

1. Personal mudslinging marked this campaign.
2. Because the vote in the Electoral College resulted in a tie, the election was settled in the House of Representatives.
3. After six days of deadlock, representatives cast their thirty-sixth ballot. The outcome: Jefferson won with ten votes.

THE ISSUES

	Jefferson (Republican)	Adams (Federalist)
Foreign	For conciliation	Federalists favored war with France but Adams opposed it
Economic	Against government help for finance, trade, or industry	For Hamilton's financial policies and government banking
Social	Champion of the Bill of Rights	Suppressed domestic criticism with Alien and Sedition Acts

QUOTES & CUSTOMS

On the Presidency "Never did a prisoner released from his chains feel such relief as I shall on shaking off the shackles of power."

On the White House "A great stone house, big enough for two emperors, one pope, and the Grand Lama in the bargain."

On Shaking Hands Jefferson originated the custom of shaking hands with the President at a White House reception on July 4, 1801. Before that, people bowed to the President.

THE LESSONS

1. The election of 1800 proved that the original electoral system would not work. The solution was the Twelfth Amendment (1804) that required electors to vote separately for President and Vice-President.
2. Peaceful transfer of power between candidates of opposing political parties was possible in a republic.

Jefferson Brings Peace, Prosperity in 1804

THE CANDIDATES

Thomas Jefferson, the incumbent Republican President, had just avoided war by persuading Congress to pass an Embargo Act to preserve American neutrality. **George Clinton** of New York was the Vice-Presidential candidate.

Charles C. Pinckney was again chosen by the Federalists as their candidate for President. **Rufus King** of New York was the Vice-Presidential candidate.

THE CAMPAIGN

1. 1804 was the first election held after ratification of the Twelfth Amendment. As a result, the Electoral College required electors to cast separate votes for President and Vice-President.
2. For the first time a majority of states selected electors by popular vote rather than by legislative choices.
3. The campaign was boring because the Federalist Party was weak and no real issues divided public opinion.

THE ISSUES

	Jefferson (Republican)	Pinckney (Federalist)
Foreign	For peace; Louisiana Purchase	Weak party policy
Economic	For prosperity, agricultural	For commercial expansion development
Social	Burr scandal (duel and alleged treason)	Lacked strong leadership; split popular opinion

QUOTES & CUSTOMS

On the Presidency "I am tired of [this] office…that brings nothing but increasing drudgery and daily loss of friends."

Final Parting Words Jefferson wrote his own epitaph which read "…Thomas Jefferson, author of the Declaration of Independence and the statute of Virginia for religious freedom, and the Father of the University of Virginia." He never once mentioned being President of the United States.

Library After the Library of Congress was burned during the War of 1812, Jefferson donated his own books to begin a new national library.

THE LESSONS

1. Peace, prosperity, charisma, and the lack of organized opposition are guarantees of reelection.

Madison, Last Founding Father, Wins in 1808

THE CANDIDATES

James Madison, Jefferson's Secretary of State and friend, was strongly endorsed by Jefferson and nominated by the Democratic-Republicans. **George Clinton** of New York was chosen to continue his work as Vice-President.

Charles C. Pinckney and **Rufus King** were selected again by the even weaker Federalist party.

THE CAMPAIGN

1. Campaign slogans became very popular, especially those having to do with "The Great Embargo." This limerick was popular: "Our ships all in motion once whitened the ocean they sailed and returned with a cargo now doomed to decay they are fallen a prey to Jefferson, worms, and EMBARGO."

THE ISSUES

	Madison (Republican)	Pinckney (Federalist)
Foreign	Favored economic sanctions, like the embargo against Britain, and sympathized with France	Favored Britain
Economic	For holding the line on taxes	For raising taxes for defense
Social	Favored agricultural interests	Strong advocates of commerce
Personal	There is no record that Madison ever attacked Pinckney	Hamilton charged Madison was the leader of a "subversive" and "dangerous" party

QUOTES & CUSTOMS

Bill of Rights James Madison wrote nine of the ten amendments in the Bill of Rights.

First Lady In 1794, Madison married the pretty Dolley Payne Todd, who charmed one and all. Dolley had also served as White House hostess for the widower Thomas Jefferson.

Classified After his death, Dolley sold Madison's secret notes on the Constitutional Convention to the government.

THE LESSONS

1. Madison, called the Father of the Constitution, proved with Jefferson that Democratic-Republican leadership would not result in mob rule, despite Federalist fears.

Madison Struggles with War and Wins in 1812

THE CANDIDATES

James Madison, the incumbent Democratic-Republican President, was leading the nation in war against Great Britain. **Elbridge Gerry,** the "Gentleman Democrat" from Massachusetts and a signer of the Declaration of Independence, was selected as Vice-Presidential candidate.

DeWitt Clinton, mayor of New York and originally a Republican, was selected as Federalist choice for President. **Jared Ingersoll,** a Philadelphia lawyer, was chosen for Vice-President.

THE CAMPAIGN

1. The election of 1812 was the last time the Federalist party would select a Presidential candidate.
2. In the midst of war, Madison won decisively with an electoral vote of 128 to 89.

THE ISSUES

	Madison (Republican)	Clinton (Federalist)
Foreign	Directed the War of 1812 with only ten thousand troops and less than two dozen ships in the beginning	Against the War of 1812, calling it "Mr. Madison's War"
Economic	Wanted to restrict free trade to coerce France and Britain	Against wartime trade restrictions
Social	Drew support from people in the South and West	Became a regional party of Northeastern supporters

QUOTES & CUSTOMS

Pocket Veto President Madison was the first President to exercise the pocket veto, refusing to act on a naturalization bill in 1812.

Famous Sayings The War of 1812 provided us with now famous quotations. "Don't give up the ship," said U.S. Captain James Lawrence while dying aboard the USS Chesapeake in 1813. "We have met the enemy, and they are ours," said Captain Oliver Hazard Perry upon winning the battle of Lake Erie in 1813.

White House After the War of 1812, the Executive Mansion was painted white to cover the scorched exterior. Ever after, it has been called the White House.

THE LESSONS

1. No President since Madison has failed to win reelection in wartime.

Monroe Leads Era of Good Feelings in 1816

THE CANDIDATES

James Monroe, as Madison's Secretary of State and Secretary of War, was his personal choice as well as the Democratic-Republican party's choice for the fifth President of the United States. **Daniel Tompkins,** New York governor, was selected as Vice-Presidential candidate.

Rufus King was not officially selected by the Federalists, but as a former official nominee for Vice-President he was supported by the electors from Massachusetts, Connecticut, and Delaware. All others voted for Madison.

THE CAMPAIGN

1. The Federalist party died out, and the Democratic-Republican party enjoyed widespread popularity.
2. Monroe was held in high esteem and won with an electoral vote of 183 to King's 34.

THE ISSUES

	Monroe (Republican)	King (Federalist)
Foreign	As Secretary of War, Monroe inspired the troops; as President, he maintained a larger peacetime army and navy	End of War of 1812 brought peace and the end of the Federalist party
Economic	For the growth of commerce and industry, a protective tariff, and the American system	No policy
Social	Era of Good Feelings following the war unified North, South, and West	No issues during a time of prosperity

QUOTES & CUSTOMS

Monrovia Liberia is the only foreign country to have its capital, Monrovia, named after an American President—Monroe.

Happy Days The essence of the "good feelings" surrounding Monroe's election were captured in his inaugural address: "Never did a government commence under auspices so favorable nor ever was success so complete….[In] history, we find no example of a growth so rapid, so gigantic, of a people so prosperous and happy."

THE LESSONS

1. The two-party system could lead the country with responsible leadership in a nonpartisan fashion.
2. More than party organizations, leaders have the important job of cultivating talent and virtue.

THE CANDIDATES

James Monroe and his Vice-President, **Daniel D. Tompkins,** became the Republican candidates for reelection when the Democratic-Republican caucus failed to make nominations.

The Era of Good Feelings continued with increased prosperity. Monroe ran unopposed and received the electoral votes of all but one since the Electoral College wanted to preserve the honor of unanimity for George Washington.

THE CAMPAIGN

1. In the absence of an opposing candidate, no campaign issues demanded the public's attention.

THE ISSUES

	Monroe (Republican)	(Federalist)
Foreign	Threat of European aggression in South America led to the Monroe Doctrine	
Economic	Recession began in 1819 and renewed popular criticism of the national bank	
Social	Slavery issue resulted in the Missouri Compromise	
Personal	Jefferson described Monroe as "a man whose soul might be turned wrong side outwards without discovering a blemish to the world."	

QUOTES & CUSTOMS

On Slavery Monroe promoted the colonizing of Liberia, Africa by free blacks.

Monroe Doctrine The 1823 policy warned the world, "the American continents, by the free and independent condition which they have assumed and maintained, are henceforth not to be considered as subjects for future colonization by any European powers."

THE LESSONS

1. Even the depression of 1819 and the tremendous federal deficit of 1820 did not affect the election.

2. As a result of the general sense of well-being, Monroe was swept into an unopposed second term despite economic recession and foreign concerns.

3. Everyone assumed Monroe would not run for a third term because of Washington's example. By now it was traditional for the Secretary of State to run for President. John Quincy Adams was Monroe's expected successor.

THE CANDIDATES

John Quincy Adams was the first President to be elected without receiving a majority of the popular or electoral vote.

William H. Crawford of Georgia claimed to represent Jefferson's ideas.

Andrew Jackson of Tennessee enjoyed widespread popular support.

Henry Clay of Kentucky was Speaker of the House and champion of the "American system."

All candidates were considered Republicans, since the Federalist Party was dead.

THE CAMPAIGN

1. When the Republican caucus in Congress met, it chose Crawford as the Presidential candidate. State caucuses ignored Congress and chose Adams, Jackson, and Clay.

2. After popular and electoral votes were counted, no candidate had a majority.

3. According to Article II of the Constitution, the House of Representatives then had to select the new President. Clay, with the fewest electoral votes, had to drop out. He met with Adams; later, Clay's supporters voted for Adams who won.

4. Jackson and Crawford screamed "corrupt bargain," and Jacksonians began a long campaign for 1828.

THE ISSUES

	Adams (Republican)	Jackson (Republican)
Foreign	For protective tariffs	For tariff to expand our markets
Economic	For internal improvements at national expense	For roads to link trade with west and coast
Social	Antislavery	For states' rights on slavery

QUOTES & CUSTOMS

Photogenic J. Q. Adams is the first President of whom a photograph exists.

Swimmer On warm mornings, Adams liked to swim in the Potomac River. One day a reporter Anne Royall, surprised him at the river. She sat on his clothes until he promised to grant her an interview. She got it.

THE LESSONS

1. The unpopular reaction to Clay's appointment as Secretary of State after throwing his support to Adams taught politicians that the illusion of corruption can ruin a political career.

2. Although no one was better prepared for the Presidency by education or political experience, Adams's "cold, austere, and forbidding manners" did not make him a popular leader.

Jackson Leads Democrats to Victory in 1828

THE CANDIDATES

Andrew Jackson pursued the office of the President with great determination and the backing of the newly formed Democratic Party. **John C. Calhoun** was his Vice-Presidential candidate.

John Quincy Adams, the incumbent Republican President, and his Vice-President, **Henry Clay,** struggled with corruption charges and suffered from the lack of support.

THE CAMPAIGN

1. The 1828 election was the first in which Presidential nominations were made by state legislatures rather than congressional caucuses.
2. The Jacksonians called themselves Democrats, while the former Federalists joined with the Adams-Clay faction to create the National Republican party.
3. In 1828, Jackson made one of the first campaign tours, traveling to New Orleans.

THE ISSUES

	Jackson (Democrat)	Adams (Republican)
Foreign	Was accused of having no experience as a statesman	For a protective tariff
Economic	Against federally funded internal improvements; for state banks	For federal funding for internal improvements and a national bank
Social	Emphasized states' rights	For federal leadership
Personal	Was criticized for the circumstances surrounding his marriage when his wife's divorce was not official	Despite personal integrity, was accused of corrupt politics in the 1824 election

QUOTES & CUSTOMS

Spoils System Despite the slogan "To the winner belong the spoils," Jackson replaced only one-sixth of federal office-holders while President.

Kitchen Cabinet Barely on speaking terms with most of his cabinet, Jackson relied on informal advisors known as the "Kitchen Cabinet."

On the Union Jackson toasted the Union, saying, "Our Union: it must be preserved." Arch-rival Calhoun responded, "The Union: next to our liberty, most dear."

THE LESSONS

1. The two-party system became a fact of American politics.
2. Jacksonian Democracy came to represent the beliefs and energy of the common people.
3. Campaigning took on new dimensions with popular songs and staged parades, barbecues, and dinners to rally voters.

Jackson Unites the Country in 1832

THE CANDIDATES

Andrew Jackson, the incumbent President, and his choice for Vice-President, **Martin Van Buren,** rode a wave of popular support that led to an overwhelming victory for the Democrats.

Henry Clay, John Adams's Vice-President, campaigned as the National Republican candidate on the policies followed by Adams. The party's Vice-Presidential candidate was **John Sergeant** of Pennsylvania.

THE CAMPAIGN

1. Political cartoons were used extensively.
2. For the first time, national party conventions selected candidates.
3. Jackson won a smashing victory with 219 electoral votes to Clay's 49. Popular vote was closer with 687,502 for Jackson, 530,189 for Clay.

THE ISSUES

	Jackson (Democrat)	Clay (Republican)
Foreign	For tariff laws; provoked France in an attempt to collect an old debt	For a protective tariff
Economic	Vetoed bill to recharter the bank of the United States	For the national bank and Federally sponsored internal improvements
Social	Against nullification; Indian rights ignored	Referred to common people as the "great unwashed"
Personal	Jackson was criticized for his duels, fights, and habits, like not going to church on Sunday	The National Republicans were called "corrupt aristocrats"

QUOTES & CUSTOMS

Born in U.S.A. Born of immigrant parents, Jackson became the only first-generation American to become President.

Traveler Jackson become the first President to ride on a railroad train, twelve miles.

Assassination Attempt The first attempt to assassinate a President happened on January 30, 1835. Richard Laurence shot two pistols at Jackson, but miraculously both guns misfired.

Dueling Jackson was involved in over one hundred duels; Madison and Lincoln, one apiece.

THE LESSONS

1. Two-party campaigns created higher voter turnout than the one-party campaigns.
2. Jackson proved that a candidate can take a solid stand on a controversial issue and still be elected.

Van Buren, the Magician, Wins in 1836

THE CANDIDATES

Martin Van Buren, Andrew Jackson's Vice President and political heir, had **Richard M. Johnson** of Kentucky as his Vice-President. They rode on Jackson's prestige to carry on for the Democrats.

William Henry Harrison, Daniel Webster, and **Hugh T. White** ran as regional candidates for the newly formed Whig party supported by former Republicans.

THE CAMPAIGN

1. Opposition to Van Buren was widespread but divided.
2. Johnson angered Southern society by claiming equality for his part-black daughters.
3. Since no Vice-Presidential candidate received a majority of electoral votes, the Senate for the first and only time selected the Vice-President, Johnson.

THE ISSUES

	Van Buren (Democrat)	Harrison (Whig)
Foreign	Against protective tariff businesses	For tariffs to protect American businesses
Economic	Against national bank; for independent treasury system and paper money;	For national bank; blamed for the Panic of 1837
Social	For ten-hour workday	Emphasized the federal government to unify the regions

QUOTES & CUSTOMS

What Do You Think? Van Buren was very reticent about giving an opinion. Once asked, "Fine day, isn't it, Mr. Van Buren?" he replied, "Now that depends on what you mean by a fine day."

Caretaker As evidence that he intended to follow in Jackson's footsteps, Van Buren reappointed all the members of Jackson's cabinet.

THE LESSONS

1. National organization, a national candidate, and a national issue are keys to Presidential campaign success.

Harrison Wins Short-Lived Presidency in 1840

THE CANDIDATES

William Henry Harrison, an old war hero in the Battle of Tippecanoe, and **John Tyler** of Virginia led the Whig fight against the Democrats.

Martin Van Buren, the incumbent President, ran alone because the Democratic convention could not agree on a Vice-President and decided to leave the choice to the electors.

THE CAMPAIGN

1. Democrats campaigned with the slogan "Tippecanoe and Tyler too." Harrison was a log-cabin and hard-cider candidate, despite the fact he lived in a mansion.
2. Harrison was the first candidate to "take to the stump" and give speeches in various parts of the country.
3. In 1840, 78 percent of all eligible voters went to the polls, the highest ever. It was the first election in which a candidate got over a million votes.
4. President for only thirty-one days, Harrison was the first President to die in office. He developed pneumonia after giving a two-hour inauguration speech, on a cold, rainy day standing without coat, gloves, or hat.

THE ISSUES

	Harrison (Whig)	Van Buren (Democrat)
Foreign	For protective tariff	For immigration and the "asylum of the oppressed"
Economic	For the reestablishment of a national bank	Blamed for the national depression
Social	Ignored issues	For strict interpretation of Constitution; ignored the issue of slavery

QUOTES & CUSTOMS

Shopping President Harrison used to do the family grocery shopping with a basket on his arm.

In the Family William Henry Harrison was the grandfather of another President, Benjamin Harrison.

Spoils System Harrison was harassed by Whig Office-seekers. Senator Clay came seeking jobs for his friends and was kicked out of the White House when Harrison warned him, "You are too impetuous."

Dying Words "Sir, I wish you to understand the true principles of the government. I wish them carried out."

THE LESSONS

1. Songs, slogans, hoopla, and an inoffensive candidate can be propelled by a national party into the Presidency.
2. Apparent criticisms, like the "log-cabin and hard-cider" remark, can be turned into a political advantage.

Polk, the "Dark Horse," Wins in 1844

THE CANDIDATES

James K. Polk and George M. Dallas of Pennsylvania took advantage of incumbent President John Tyler's unpopularity and the Democrats' strong organization.

Henry Clay, the Whig nominee, ran with Senator **Theodore Frelinghuysen** of New Jersey on a conservative, though vague, platform.

James G. Birney of Michigan and **Thomas Morris** of Ohio ran as Liberty party candidates favoring abolition of slavery.

THE CAMPAIGN

1. Polk's selection as nominee for the Democratic party marked the first time a party selected a "dark-horse" (a long-shot) candidate.
2. When the Democrats nominated Polk, Andrew Jackson urged Tyler to withdraw so the party could concentrate on defeating Clay and not split the popular vote.

THE ISSUES

	Polk (Democrat)	Clay (Whig)	Birney (Liberty)
Foreign	For annexation of Texas and the Oregon Territory	For annexation of Texas	Against annexation of Texas
Economic	For revenue tariffs; against national bank	For protective tariffs	For balanced tax
Social	For states' rights on slavery	Proslavery	Antislavery
Personal	Sam Houston complained Polk "drank too much water"	Branded a gambler, a duelist, and a corrupt bargainer	

QUOTES & CUSTOMS

On the Presidency Polk believed "The Chief Magistrate...should not be the President of a part only, but of the whole people of the United States."

Campaign Promises Polk promised to acquire California, settle the Oregon dispute, lower the tariff, start a sub-treasury, and retire after 4 years. He did everything he promised!

Another Promise Andrew Jackson promised his niece, Sarah Childress, "Daughter, I will put you in the White House if it costs me my life." He did. She married James K. Polk.

THE LESSONS

1. Tyler's stubborn independence alienated him from his party and left him a political orphan.
2. Candidates prefer to ignore controversial issues, but taxes and slavery demanded reluctant attention.

Taylor, Another War Hero, Wins in 1848

THE CANDIDATES

Zachary Taylor, the Whig candidate, with forty years in the army and no political experience, ran with **Millard Fillmore** of New York, who became the thirteenth President after Taylor's death.

Lewis Cass, the candidate of a deeply divided Democratic party, was a senator from Michigan who had served under General Andrew Jackson. His Vice-Presidential candidate was **General William O. Butler** of Kentucky.

THE CAMPAIGN

1. Slavery became the major issue of this election and every election until the Civil War.
2. Whigs and Democrats counted on "party regulars," who voted along party lines regardless of the candidate's character or principles.
3. The Democratic Party divided into proslavery and antislavery factions.
4. Taylor never voted in a Presidential election before 1848, when he voted for himself.

THE ISSUES

	Taylor (Whig)	Cass (Democrat)
Foreign	For war with Mexico, annexation of Texas	Justified war with Mexico
Economic	For payment of national debt, less government spending, no patronage, cheap postage	Against a national bank; for the repeal of the Tariff of 1842
Social	For free labor and free soil for a free people	Against Wilmot Proviso; pro-Union
Personal	Polk called Taylor "undereducated, exceedingly ignorant of public affairs, and of very ordinary capacity"	Critics feared wars of aggression against smaller countries

QUOTES & CUSTOMS

On Taking Office D. R. Atchison, pro tem Speaker of the House, became President for one day because Taylor refused to be sworn into office on a Sunday.

White House Manners Taylor chewed tobacco and was known as a "sure-shot spitter"; he never missed the sawdust box in the White House.

All in the Family Taylor's daughter, Sarah, wanted to marry the dashing lieutenant on her father's staff. Sarah married Jefferson Davis despite her family's opposition.

Last Words After suffering from heat stroke on July 4, 1850, Taylor died five days later, saying, "God knows that I have endeavored to fulfill what I conceived to be my honest duty."

THE LESSONS

1. Both parties learned to attract new voters and to take advantage of a divided opposition.
2. The public does not require political experience from popular war-hero candidates for the Presidency.

Pierce Leads a Landslide Victory in 1852

THE CANDIDATES

Franklin Pierce, the Democratic dark-horse candidate from New Hampshire, was selected on the forty-ninth ballot. Pierce united both wings of his party. Senator **William R. King** of Alabama was the Vice-Presidential nominee.

Winfield Scott, a Mexican War hero called Old Fuss and Feathers, gained the Whig nomination on the fifty-third ballot. His running mate, Secretary of the Navy **William A. Graham,** was a rare Unionist Southerner.

THE CAMPAIGN

1. Whigs dumped the non-elected incumbent President Fillmore for the lure of the war-hero candidate.
2. The issue of slavery dominated the politics of the country.
3. Mrs. Pierce fainted when she heard the news her husband was nominated. Mrs. Pierce did not attend the inauguration.

THE ISSUES

	Pierce (Democrat)	Scott (Whig)
Foreign	For friendly relations with Mexico	Avoided entangling alliances
Economic	For paying national debt and internal improvements	For strict economy with government revenue raised from duty on imports
Social	For Compromise of 1850, extension of slavery	For Compromise of 1850, strict enforcement of Fugitive Slave Law

QUOTES & CUSTOMS

On His Nomination "You're looking at the most surprised man that ever lived."

The White House During Pierce's stay in the White House, central heating was installed.

Campaign Slogan "We Polked 'em in '44, and we'll Pierce 'em in '52."

THE LESSONS

1. Personal tragedy can undermine political self-confidence and effectiveness.
2. The election of 1852 gave the death blow to the divided and leaderless Whig Party, which was unable to cope with the vital issue of the day, slavery.
3. War heroes do not always win elections.

Buchanan Struggles with Division in 1856

THE CANDIDATES

John Buchanan was "the most available and most unobjectionable" choice of the Democrats. He had served as Secretary of State and as minister to England. His service in England had protected him from the slavery controversy. Representative **John C. Breckinridge,** his Vice-Presidential candidate, later ran for the Presidency in the 1860 election.

John C. Frémont, "the Pathfinder," was the candidate of the new Republican party which opposed the extension of slavery. He ran with **William L. Dayton,** a former senator for New Jersey, as his Vice-Presidential candidate.

THE CAMPAIGN

1. The incredible sum of one million dollars was spent on the combined campaigns.
2. The Whig party, allied with the Know-Nothings, campaigned for Fillmore and won only the state of Maryland.
3. This campaign and election emphasized the split in the country. Frémont carried the free states, Buchanan all but one slave state.

THE ISSUES

	Buchanan (Democrat)	Frémont (Republican)
Foreign	For free seas, progressive free trade, and Monroe Doctrine in Gulf of Mexico	Against Ostend Manifesto
Economic	Against a national bank; for a separate treasury, internal improvements	For railroad to Pacific, federal funds
Social	For citizenship for aliens; against congressional interference in slavery issue	Against extension of slavery, regional parties

QUOTES & CUSTOMS

Hospitality When the Prince of Wales visited the White House, he was quartered in Buchanan's room; Buchanan slept on the sofa.

On First Ladies Buchanan was our only bachelor President. His niece, Harriet, served as his hostess.

Campaign Rhetoric When an Englishman told Buchanan that the newspapers led him to suppose the Presidential candidates must be the greatest rascals in America, he replied, "It did look so, but it was only a way we had of talking."

THE LESSONS

1. The South made it clear that it would secede if a purely Northern party won the Presidency.
2. The United States could no longer delude itself that the slavery issue was settled by the Compromise of 1850.

Lincoln Leads a Divided Nation in 1860

THE CANDIDATES

Abraham Lincoln from Illinois won the Republican party nomination by acclamation. His running mate was Senator **Hannibal Hamlin** of Maine.

Stephen A. Douglas, Democratic candidate and senator from Illinois, adhered to the theory of "popular sovereignty." He was supported by Northern Democrats, and his Vice-Presidential candidate was Senator **Benjamin Fitzpatrick** of Alabama.

John Breckinridge of Kentucky ran as a candidate for the Southern Democratic party.

John Bell, former Speaker of the House, represented the Constitutional Union party, made up of Whigs and Know-Nothings.

THE CAMPAIGN

1. In the first Presidential campaign in which a candidate made national tours, Douglas traveled five thousand miles. Lincoln, confident that the split in the Democratic party would give him victory, stayed in Illinois.
2. Americans voted along sectional lines. Lincoln carried eighteen free states.

THE ISSUES

	Lincoln (Republican)	Douglas (Democrat)
Foreign	Against acquisition of Cuba as extension of "slavocracy"	For acquisition of Cuba and Mexico
Economic	For industry, fair wages for labor	For transcontinental railroad
Social	For preserving the Union	For the Fugitive Slave Laws
Personal	*Harper's Weekly* called Lincoln uneducated, a vulgar village politician, "a horrid looking wretch"	Described by opponents as morally deficient, egotistic, and condescending

QUOTES & CUSTOMS

Campaign Appearances "Well, Mary, if nothing else comes out of this scrape, we are going to have some new clothes."

On Gifts Lincoln was offered several dozen elephants by the King of Siam. He refused the gift, but the elephant became the symbol of the Republican party.

Inaugural Address "I have no purpose... to interfere with the institution of slavery in the states where it exists."

THE LESSONS

1. The federal union must be preserved.
2. The Republican party won its first Presidential election.
3. A divided party increases the probability of the opposing party's victory.

Lincoln Still Fights for the Union in 1864

THE CANDIDATES

Abraham Lincoln, the incumbent Republican President, ran with **Andrew Johnson,** a former senator and military governor of Tennessee, instead of the incumbent Hamlin. Johnson became the seventeenth President in 1865 after Lincoln's assassination, but he barely survived impeachment proceedings.

George B. McClellan, the Democratic candidate, was a former commanding general of the Union forces who had been relieved by the President in 1862 for his failure to act to win the war. His running mate was **George H. Pendleton** of Ohio.

THE CAMPAIGN

1. Voters showed a reluctance to turn an incumbent out of office during wartime.
2. Soldiers away from home voted by absentee ballot.

THE ISSUES

	Lincoln (Republican)	McClellan (Democrat)
Foreign	Blockaded South to prevent British trade; for immigration	For British support in Civil War, acquisition of Cuba
Economic	For war effort	Limited resources exceeded demands of prolonged war
Social	Proclaimed authority of Constitution and U.S. law; demanded unconditional surrender	For ending Civil War, preserving the federal union with states' rights unimpaired

QUOTES & CUSTOMS

On Reelection Lincoln quipped, "It is not good policy to swap horses while crossing a stream."

Second Inaugural Address "With malice toward none, with charity for all, with firmness in the right as God gives us to see the light, let us strive on to finish the work we are in, to bind up the nation's wounds... to do all which may achieve and cherish a just and lasting peace."

THE LESSONS

1. A people's government can hold a national election even in the midst of great civil war.
2. Despite the most intense character assassination marking a campaign so far, common sense prevailed.
3. Two political parties, the Democrats and the Republicans, emerged and continue to dominate U.S. politics.

Grant Battles with Politics in 1868

THE CANDIDATES

Ulysses S. Grant, nominated unanimously on the first roll call by the Republicans, was the victorious leader of the Union Army during the Civil War. The fact that he was not a politician only increased his popularity. Running for Vice-President was **Schuyler Colfax** of Indiana, the Speaker of the House.

Horatio Seymour, Democrat, was so reluctant to accept the nomination of his party that he was called The Great Decliner. His running mate was **General Francis P. Blair, Jr.,** of Missouri.

THE CAMPAIGN

1. From 1868 until the end of the century, Republican politicians would "wave the bloody shirt," meaning they would blame the South for the Civil War and the loss of so many men.
2. Grant refused to campaign.

THE ISSUES

	Grant (Republican)	Seymour (Democrat)
Foreign	For same treatment for naturalized citizens as for native born	For protection of all naturalized citizens
Economic	For rapid and equal reduction of taxes, payment of public debt	For wide distribution of public lands, uniform currency, equal taxation, and paying national debt
Social	For equal civil and political rights	For states' rights, regulation of suffrage

QUOTES & CUSTOMS

Peace Grant added the line "Let us have peace" when signing his acceptance, and it became his campaign slogan.

On Music "I know only two tunes. One of them is 'Yankee Doodle' and the other one isn't."

Stage-struck During the War with Mexico, bored soldiers staged Shakespeare's Othello. Grant played Desdemona.

THE LESSONS

1. The black vote was crucial to the triumph of Grant at the polls; the Republicans urged passage of the Fifteenth Amendment (1870) protecting Negro suffrage.
2. Because of the Greenback issue, business people voted with the Republican party, which has been their political home ever since.
3. This election made it clear that the South would play an important role in politics.

Grant Fights in Mud in 1872

THE CANDIDATES

Ulysses S. Grant, chosen by acclamation of the Republicans, would be hounded by corruption and nepotism, although he was personally honest. His Vice-Presidential candidate was **Senator Henry Wilson** of Massachusetts.

Horace Greeley, nominee of both the Liberal Republicans (dissatisfied with Grant) and the Democrats, was the editor of the New York Tribune. His running mate was **B. Gratz Brown,** governor of Missouri. The Democrats accepted these men as their candidates.

THE CAMPAIGN

1. Greeley departed from the usual custom by going "on the stump" and actively campaigning.
2. A new word, Grantism, was coined to describe the nepotism, the spoils system, and the hopeless incompetence of Grant's administration.
3. Susan B. Anthony decided the Fourteenth Amendment gave her the right to vote. She voted in Rochester, New York, on November 5, 1872, and was arrested.

THE ISSUES

	Grant (Republican)	Greeley (Democrat)
Foreign	For worldwide respect	For friendship with other countries through fair treaties
Economic	For a uniform national currency, higher import duties, giving public land to settlers	For reducing high tariff, federal taxation; against land grants to railroads
Social	Corruption rampant; for pensions for war veterans, humane policy toward Indians, rights for women	For reforming civil service, honoring veterans, withdrawing federal troops from the South

QUOTES & CUSTOMS

Making Mistakes Grant acknowledged, "Mistakes have been made, as all can see and I admit."

Memories Facing cancer and bankruptcy, Grant wrote his personal memoirs, finishing it just days before his death. Mark Twain had the memoirs published, and it earned about $500,000.

On Exercise On first visiting a golf course, Grant saw a novice vigorously swinging a club. "That does look like very good exercise," said Grant. "What is the little white ball for?"

THE LESSONS

1. In most states, a Republican "boss" exercised power to dispense patronage and appoint to office those who served political interests.
2. The Prohibition party made its first appearance in this election year. It ultimately secured the Eighteenth Amendment (1919).
3. Despite the Fourteenth and Fifteenth Amendments, the civil rights of black people were severely restricted.

Hayes Wins Despite Tilden's Election in 1876

THE CANDIDATES

Rutherford B. Hayes was nominated by the scandal-ridden Republican party as an upright political leader who was also a general in the Union Army. Running for Vice-President was Representative **William A. Wheeler** of New York.

Samuel J. Tilden was a reform candidate who had sent the notorious Boss Tweed to jail. He shared the ticket with **Thomas A. Hendricks,** governor of Indiana, who had been the runner-up for the Presidential nomination.

THE CAMPAIGN

1. After a bitter campaign, Tilden received 4,284,020 popular votes to Hayes's 4,036,572.

2. The Republicans challenged the returns in South Carolina, Florida, Louisiana, and Oregon to give Hayes a narrow one vote electoral margin of victory.

3. A special Electoral Commission handed the Presidency to Hayes by a vote of eight to seven. In return for the Commission vote, Hayes agreed to withdraw troops from the South. The House approved Hayes just 56 hours before the inauguration.

THE ISSUES

	Hayes (Republican)	Tilden (Democrat)
Foreign	For treaties to protect naturalized citizens	For treaty with China to restrict labor
Economic	For ending depression with sound money and gold standard, increasing imports; against granting public land to corporations	For a sound currency with silver restructured tax system; against tariff
Social	For public school system, women's rights; against sectionalism	For reform of civil service, state supported public schools

QUOTES & CUSTOMS

Last Annual Message Hayes asked for a building for the Library of Congress and the completion of the Washington Monument.

On Temperance Hayes's last executive order banned the sale of liquor at army camps and forts. During his administration, no alcoholic beverages were served at the White House, and his wife was nicknamed "Lemonade Lucy."

THE LESSONS

1. With the removal of federal troops, federal support for black civil rights ended.

2. The disputed election resulted in the passage of the Electoral Commission Law of 1877, which regulates the counting of votes for the President and Vice-President.

3. Both parties were so appalled at the depth and extent of the corruption under the Grant administrations that they both called for extensive reform.

Garfield Wins, but Arthur Leads After 1880

THE CANDIDATES

James A. Garfield, the dark-horse candidate of the Republicans, won the nomination on the thirty-sixth ballot. For Vice-President, the nominee was **Chester A. Arthur** who would become the twenty-first President in 1881, upon Garfield's assassination.

Winfield S. Hancock, a Gettysburg war hero, was nominated by the Democrats. Running with him was former representative from Indiana, **William H. English.**

THE CAMPAIGN

1. The nickname G.O.P., which stands for "Grand Old Party," was widely used for the first time at the 1880 Republican convention.

2. For the first time a Presidential nominee (Garfield) was present at the convention.

3. In 1881, we had three Presidents: Hayes's term ended March 3; Garfield died in September; Arthur succeeded him.

THE ISSUES

	Garfield (Republican)	Hancock (Democrat)
Foreign	For restricted immigration; against Chinese immigration	Against Chinese immigration
Economic	For protective tariff	Against protective tariff; for "honest" money—gold, silver, or paper convertible to coin on demand
Social	For federal aid to states for public education, civil-service reform	Against government reform by statute

QUOTES & CUSTOMS

On Getting Ahead Garfield claimed "A pound of pluck is worth a ton of luck."

On the White House "My God! What is there in this place that a man should want to get in it?"

On His Death Garfield served only two hundred days as President, and for eighty of these days he lay near death. Hayes said of him, "He is the ideal self-made man."

Talented Garfield, once a college president, could write Greek with one hand and, at the same time, Latin with the other.

THE LESSONS

1. The eleven former Confederate states would no longer automatically vote Republican.

2. Garfield's assassination lent impetus to demands for civil-service reform. He was shot by a disappointed office-seeker.

Cleveland Wins for the Democrats in 1884

THE CANDIDATES

Grover Cleveland, governor of New York, was the nominee of the Democrats and supported by liberal Republicans, called Mugwumps, committed to reform. **Governor Thomas A. Hendricks** of Indiana was his running mate.

James G. Blaine was the most popular Republican of his generation but tainted with railroad scandals. His running mate was Ohioan **Thomas Hendricks.** Unfortunately he died after only a few months in office.

THE CAMPAIGN

1. For the first time, the Republican convention prescribed how and when delegates should be selected, instead of inviting all interested parties.
2. The chief issues in the 1884 campaign were Blaine's public dishonesty and Cleveland's private immorality.
3. Democrats, enraged over the "rum, Romanism, and rebellion" remark made by Blaine supporters, carried the New York vote and, with it, the election.

THE ISSUES

	Cleveland (Democrat)	Blaine (Republican)
Foreign	For low protective tariff, restoring naval strength	For high protective tariff, strong Latin American policy
Economic	For regulation of railways, international gold standard, regulation of interstate commerce; against free silver	For reducing taxation, promoting U.S. industry, improvement of the Mississippi River, revocation of land grants to railway corporations
Social	For a national bureau of labor, eight-hour workday, public education, civil-service reform	For civil-service reform, free action by labor

QUOTES & CUSTOMS

Cleveland's Campaign Slogan "Public Office is a Public Trust."

Money Cleveland's portrait appears on the thousand-dollar bill.

Appearance Cleveland, weighing in at 260 pounds, was called "Uncle Jumbo."

Weddings Cleveland was the first President to marry while in the White House and the first President to have his child born there.

THE LESSONS

1. The South voted Democratic to elect the first Democratic President since 1856. The Solid South continued to do so for a hundred years.
2. The candidate who did the least campaigning won the election. The candidate who campaigned for six weeks and made four hundred speeches lost.

Harrison Wins with Minority Vote in 1888

THE CANDIDATES

Benjamin Harrison, Republican grandson of President William Henry Harrison, fulfilled two important Republican qualifications: he was a Civil War officer and was born in Ohio. **Levi Parsons Morton,** Republican banker and representative from New York, was backed for the Vice-Presidential spot.

Grover Cleveland, the incumbent Democratic President, had antagonized many during his first term. **Allen Granberry Thurman,** Democratic party faithful from Ohio, was selected for the Vice-Presidential position.

THE CAMPAIGN

1. Both parties used "floaters" (people who sold their votes), but the Republicans were able to "out-buy" the Democrats because of their large campaign chest.
2. Cleveland received 5,447,129 popular votes, over 100,000 more than Harrison.

THE ISSUES

	Harrison (Republican)	Cleveland (Democrat)
Foreign	For high tariffs	For low tariffs
Economic	For reduction of internal taxes	Alienated industry because of stand on tariffs
Social	For pensions for Civil War veterans, federal aid to education, civil-service reform	Vetoed pension bills for Civil War veterans

QUOTES & CUSTOMS

On the Presidency Harrison complained "I could not name my own Cabinet. They had sold out every place to pay the election expenses."

Lights Out Electric lights were installed in the White House in 1890, but the Harrisons left the job of turning them off and on to the servants.

THE LESSONS

1. The election of 1888 proved that the candidate receiving the most popular votes would not necessarily be elected President.
2. Money from big business can influence an election.

Cleveland Makes a Comeback in 1892

THE CANDIDATES

Grover Cleveland, one-term Democratic President defeated by Harrison in 1888, returned to challenge Harrison. **Adlai Ewing Stevenson,** Democrat from Illinois, was nominated for Vice-President.

Benjamin Harrison, incumbent Republican President, whose previous term had increased federal spending and admitted six new states to the Union, ran with **Whitelaw Reid,** Republican from New York.

James B. Weaver, Populist candidate from Iowa, ran with **James G. Field** from Virginia.

THE CAMPAIGN

1. Neither Harrison nor Cleveland actively campaigned.
2. The Populists provided campaign interest and enjoyed particular strength in the West.

THE ISSUES

	Cleveland (Democrat)	Harrison (Republican)	Weaver (Populist)
Foreign	Against free trade; for lower tariff, canal across Central America	For high tariff, stiff immigration laws, a canal across Central America	For restricted immigration
Economic	For gold standard, antitrust laws, inland waterways	For free rural mail delivery, bimetallism	For free coinage of silver, graduated income tax
Social	For federal aid to education	For federal aid to education, veteran pensions, civil-service reform	For social equality

QUOTES & CUSTOMS

Unique Cleveland is the only man to serve two nonconsecutive terms as president.

Friends and Enemies The man nominating Cleveland for President was quoted as saying, "We love him most for the enemies he has made."

Unconstitutional On May 20, 1895, the income tax was declared unconstitutional.

THE LESSONS

1. Although the Populist party failed to get its candidates elected, it was the only third party to carry a single state in elections between 1860 and 1912.
2. Standing firm on principles that had cost him the 1888 election, Cleveland was able to regain the Presidency.

McKinley, War Hero from Ohio, Wins in 1896

THE CANDIDATES

William McKinley, Republican governor of Ohio and Civil War hero, had sponsored the high tariff bill of 1890. **Garret Augustus Hobart** from New Jersey balanced the Republican ticket.

William Jennings Bryan won the Democratic nomination after receiving thunderous applause for one hour after his famous "cross of gold" speech. At age thirty-six he was the youngest man to be nominated for President. **Arthur Sewall,** a banker from Maine, balanced the ticket.

THE CAMPAIGN

1. McKinley's campaign manager conducted the first modern advertising campaign using cartoons and posters. Over 120 million campaign documents were distributed.
2. McKinley conducted a front-porch campaign in Canton, Ohio, and by election day over 750,000 people from 30 states had called on him at his home.
3. Telephones were used to campaign for the first time.

QUOTES & CUSTOMS

On Winning Campaign manager Mark Hanna wired McKinley, "God's in his Heaven—All's right with the world."

New Foreign Policy "Isolation is no longer possible or desirable."

On Congress Senator Shelby Cullom stated, "We have never had a President who had more influence with Congress than Mr. McKinley."

THE LESSONS

1. Mayor Tom Johnson of Cleveland summed up the 1896 campaign as "the first great protest of the American people against monopoly—the first great struggle of the masses in our country against the privileged classes."

THE ISSUES

	McKinley (Republican)	Bryan (Democrat)
Foreign	For acquisition of Hawaii, Central America	Against the protective tariff
Economic	For the gold standard	For free silver, federal income tax; against injunctions to end strikes
Social	For women's rights and "equal pay for equal work"	For Western statehood
Personal	Democrats denounce McKinley as a tool of the capitalists	Republicans painted Bryan as a radical, a demagogue, and a socialist

McKinley Reelected with Largest Vote in 1900

THE CANDIDATES

William McKinley, the Republican incumbent, laid the basis for the strong modern Presidency and world leadership. His running mate, **Theodore Roosevelt,** governor of New York, was originally judged to be too unpredictable by McKinley and party chairman Mark Hanna.

William Jennings Bryan, the Democrats' nominee for the second time, ran on two issues: silver and imperialism. **Adlai E. Stevenson** from Illinois was Vice-President during Cleveland's second term and was the candidate again.

THE CAMPAIGN

1. Both candidates were nominated on the first ballot.
2. McKinley observed the unwritten rule that incumbents do not campaign.
3. McKinley's was the greatest Republican victory since 1872.

THE ISSUES

	McKinley (Republican)	Bryan (Democrat)
Foreign	Success of the Spanish-American War made the President very popular	Against imperialism, military expansionism
Economic	For trusts and gold standard	For free silver; against trusts
Social	Practiced protectionism to help labor; condemned lynching	For the creation of a Department of Labor
Personal	Hearst's newspapers labeled McKinley as "Dollar Mark" Hanna's puppet	Newspapers revived the issue of Bryan's sanity or possible psychological imbalance

QUOTES & CUSTOMS

On Imperialism "Ah, you may be sure that there will be no jingo nonsense under my administration."

The McKinley Grip To save wear on his right hand at affairs with lengthy lines of guests, McKinley would take a man's right hand quickly and warmly before the man could grip him. Then he would pull the man along by the elbow with his left hand, release his right hand, and be ready for the next guest.

Assassination President McKinley was shot while standing in a receiving line. His first thought was to protect the assassin. As he fell he cried out, "Don't let them hurt him!"

THE LESSONS

1. The election of 1900 showed that during prosperous times an electorate will vote with the status quo.
2. A military success may increase the prestige of the incumbent.

Theodore Roosevelt for Square Deal in 1904

THE CANDIDATES

Theodore Roosevelt, the Republican who became President after McKinley's assassination in 1901, was anxious to prove his leadership. **Charles W. Fairbanks,** Republican senator from Indiana, was clearly overshadowed by Roosevelt but would again become the Vice-Presidential candidate in 1916.

Judge Alton B. Parker, conservative Chief Justice of the New York Court of Appeals, wasted little time campaigning for the Democrats. He ran with **Henry G. Davis,** Democratic senator from West Virginia, an eighty-two-year-old millionaire who was picked mainly for his money.

THE CAMPAIGN

1. Roosevelt defeated Parker by 2.5 million votes—the largest margin of victory ever recorded to that time.

THE ISSUES

	Roosevelt (Republican)	Parker (Democrat)
Foreign	For Panama Canal and Roosevelt Corollary to the Monroe Doctrine	Attacked American imperialism and Roosevelt's role as "international policeman"
Economic	For regulation of trusts, labor, and inter-state commerce	For the gold standard
Social	For Square Deal for labor and conservation of natural resources	For direct election of senators
Personal	Roosevelt was accused by J. Pulitzer of blackmailing corporations; called a madman	Parker had a reputation for caution; called "the enigma of New York"

QUOTES & CUSTOMS

On Campaigning "I am as strong as a bull moose."

Philosophy "Get action, do things, be sane; don't fritter away your time; create, act, take a place wherever you are and be somebody; get action."

Panama Canal "I took Panama without consulting the cabinet."

He Lost Roosevelt tried to have "In God We Trust" removed from coins, thinking it sacrilegious and unconstitutional.

THE LESSONS

1. The election of 1904 showed that military heroes may evolve into strong candidates.
2. An underdog cannot run a half-hearted campaign and expect to win.
3. Voters respect forceful personalities in their Presidential candidates.

Taft Carries On in 1908

THE CANDIDATES

William H. Taft, Roosevelt's Secretary of War, was assured the Republican nomination because of Roosevelt's support. **James S. Sherman,** a Republican representative from New York, was not progressive, but he did help carry the state of New York.

William J. Bryan ran on the Democratic ticket for the third time. The Vice-President candidate, **John W. Kern,** a two-time loser in the Indiana gubernatorial race, was nevertheless a great speaker.

THE CAMPAIGN

1. Taft became markedly more progressive as he took Roosevelt's advice "Hit them hard, old man."
2. Bryan carried no Northern state and only three in the West. His only other votes came from the "Solid South." This was the worst of Bryan's three defeats.

THE ISSUES

	Taft (Republican)	Bryan (Democrat)
Foreign	For dollar diplomacy, the Roosevelt Corollary	Against imperialism; for independence for the Philippines
Economic	For strong protective tariffs	For a lower tariff, more antitrust legislation, graduated income tax
Social	For "a wise and regulated Individualism"	Bryan continually asked the Populist question: "Shall the people rule?"

QUOTES & CUSTOMS

The Supreme Court The only former President to be appointed chief justice of the United States, Taft said, "Presidents come and go, but the Court goes on forever."

Experience Only Taft became President without ever having been elected to any legislative or executive office.

Big Taft was the biggest man ever to occupy the White House, over three-hundred pounds.

THE LESSONS

1. The election of 1908 showed that an incumbent President's popularity may transfer to another candidate.
2. Progressive ideas were accepted by many middle-class Americans.

Wilson Promises a New Freedom in 1912

THE CANDIDATES

Woodrow Wilson, governor of New Jersey, won the Democratic nomination with Bryan's support. **Thomas R. Marshall,** the governor of Indiana, was picked by the convention after his state helped secure Wilson's nomination.

William H. Taft, the Republican incumbent, was renominated despite Roosevelt's anger. James S. Sherman, Taft's Vice-President, was easily renominated. Sherman died on October 30, 1912, and was replaced by **Nicholas Murray Butler.**

Theodore Roosevelt, the popular ex-President, split the Republican party by forming the new Progressive party and running as a third candidate.

Eugene Debs, nominated by the Socialist Party, was a fourth significant candidate.

THE CAMPAIGN

1. Taft, convinced he would lose, did little campaigning.
2. In October, Roosevelt was shot on his way to give a speech. He was saved from the assassin's bullet by a lengthy speech he had folded in his pocket over his heart. The bullet passed through his coat, his eyeglass case, and his 200 page speech and cracked his fifth rib.

THE ISSUES

	Wilson (Democrat)	Taft (Republican)
Foreign	Denounced imperialism, as every Democratic platform since 1900 had done	For Dollar Diplomacy in Latin America
Economic	For a lower tariff, regulation of trusts	For antitrust policies, high protective tariff
Social	For labor, pure food laws	For legislation to protect the labor of women and children; against recalling judges
Personal	Wilson refused to debate Roosevelt	Taft was largely ignored

QUOTES & CUSTOMS

Wilson's Motto "Justice, and only justice, shall always be our motto."

On Foreign Affairs (in 1912) "It would be the irony of fate if my administration had to deal chiefly with foreign affairs."

On His Presidency "I am administering a great office, no doubt the greatest in the world, but it is not me, and I am not it. I am only a commissioner, in charge of its apparatus, living in its offices and taking upon myself its functions."

THE LESSONS

1. Prosperous times do not guarantee an incumbent's reelection.
2. In 1912, one of the most popular politicians in history ran on a third-party ticket and lost. Clearly, third-party success in a Presidential election is nearly impossible.

Wilson Faces World War in 1916

THE CANDIDATES

Woodrow Wilson, the incumbent Democratic President, was renominated with the slogan "He kept us out of war." He was renominated by a vote of 1092 to 1, with **Thomas Marshall** as his running mate again.

Charles Evans Hughes, the reform governor of New York, resigned his position as a U.S. Supreme Court justice in order to become the Republican candidate for President. **Charles W. Fairbanks** was selected as the Vice-Presidential candidate.

THE CAMPAIGN

1. The election was one of the closest in U.S. history. Early returns indicated Hughes would win. However, in the end, Wilson won the electoral vote by carrying California by a mere 3,800 votes.

2. Hughes went to bed election night thinking he had won. When a reporter called to ask about Hughes's reaction to the election, his valet said, "The President has retired." The reporter responded with, "When he wakes up tell him he is no longer President."

THE ISSUES

	Wilson (Democrat)	Hughes (Republican)
Foreign	Against U.S. involvement in World War I	Wanted greater respect for American neutrality
Economic	For eight-hour workday	Against union protection
Social	For women's suffrage	Moderate support for labor

QUOTES & CUSTOMS

War Message "The world must be made safe for democracy."

Mowing the Lawn To release White House groundskeepers for the war effort, the Wilsons kept sheep on the White House lawn to eat the grass. Those same sheep were shorn, and $100,000 was given the Red Cross from the sale of their wool.

Fourteen Points When Georges Clemenceau learned about Wilson's Fourteen Points, he exclaimed, "Le bon Dieu Wavait que dix!" ["The good Lord only had ten!"]

THE LESSONS

1. This campaign showed the important role that foreign affairs can play in American politics.

2. Campaign slogans do not always predict the future. Within six months of the election, Wilson asked Congress to declare war on Germany.

Harding Turns to Normalcy in 1920

THE CANDIDATE

Warren G. Harding, senator from Ohio, was picked by Republican leaders in a Chicago hotel room after the convention became deadlocked. **Governor Calvin Coolidge** was his running mate.

James M. Cox, governor of Ohio, was chosen as the Democratic candidate with **Franklin D. Roosevelt** as the Vice-Presidential candidate.

THE CAMPAIGN

1. Harding ran a front-porch campaign. He delivered speeches from his home in Marion, Ohio.

2. In contrast to Harding's style, Cox traveled more than twenty-two thousand miles across the nation giving speeches.

3. Neither candidate discussed the controversial issue of prohibition despite the passage of the Eighteenth Amendment in 1919.

4. The election was the first in which all women in the U.S. could vote for President.

THE ISSUES

	Harding (Republican)	Cox (Democrat)
Foreign	Against the League of Nations	For U.S. support for the League
Economic	For higher tariff, reduced income taxes	For Wilson's program
Social	For restricted immigration	For labor improvements

QUOTES & CUSTOMS

Normalcy "America's present need is not heroics but healing, not nostrums but normalcy; not revolution but restoration."

Qualifications "I am not fit for this office and never should have been here."

Ohio Gang Harding's friends met regularly to play poker and dispense jobs and favors. After Harding's death, numerous scandals were revealed. Harding's involvement is difficult to know because his wife destroyed all his papers after his death.

THE LESSONS

1. The election of 1920 indicated a public rejection of Wilson's idealism.

2. After the stress of war, people wanted to return to a simpler way of life. They had tired of progressive crusades.

Coolidge Wins in a Landslide in 1924

THE CANDIDATES

Calvin Coolidge, the Vice-President who became President on Harding's death, was nominated by the Republicans. **Charles G. Dawes** was nominated for Vice-President.

John W. Davis, former minister to Great Britain, was nominated by the Democrats, with **Charles W. Bryan** as his running mate.

Robert La Follette, senator and former governor of Wisconsin, was nominated by the newly formed Progressive party.

THE CAMPAIGN

1. The Democratic convention split into two factions. One supported William McAdoo and the other Al Smith, a Roman Catholic. After 102 ballots, both sides agreed to support a third candidate, John W. Davis.

2. During the campaign, the Progressive party attracted large numbers of farmers and workers hoping to gain a larger voice in the government. La Follette won 4,800,000 votes out of 29,000,000 cast, quite impressive for a third-party candidate.

THE ISSUES

	Coolidge (Republican)	Davis (Democrat)
Foreign	For the World Court, reductions in world arms production	For the League of Nations
Economic	For reduced government debt and spending	For lower tariff, income tax
Social	Against labor arbitration	Against Harding corruption

QUOTES & CUSTOMS

Another First Coolidge's inaugural address was the first to be broadcast on the radio.

Isolation "He is the first President to discover that what the American people want is to be left alone." (Will Rogers, 1924)

Business "The business of America is business."

Silent Cal "If you don't say anything, you won't be called on to repeat it."

THE LESSONS

1. Most Americans supported the laissez-faire policies of the Republican administration and viewed the nation's prosperity as a result of those policies.

2. The election also showed that millions disagreed with Republican policies and gave support to a third party.

Hoover Faces the Great Depression in 1928

THE CANDIDATES

Herbert Hoover, capable administrator of the war relief programs, was nominated by the Republicans after Coolidge refused another term. **Charles Curtis,** a Kaw Indian of Kansas, was his running mate.

Alfred Smith, the liberal, Roman Catholic governor of New York, was the Democratic nominee, with **Joseph Robinson** as his running mate.

THE CAMPAIGN

1. The Eighteenth Amendment (Prohibition) was hotly debated.

2. The Republican campaign promised "a chicken in every pot and a car in every garage."

3. Smith was a Catholic, and rumors spread that the Pope would rule the nation if Smith were elected. Hoover and Smith tried to run dignified campaigns, but many of their supporters allowed religious bigotry to play a role in the campaign.

4. Radio played an important role in this Presidential election. Smith's New York accent sounded odd to many Americans and may have hurt him in the election.

THE ISSUES

	Hoover (Republican)	Smith (Democrat)
Foreign	Against U.S. membership in the League of Nations	Supported "constructive" foreign policy
Economic	For higher tariff, continued prosperity	For lower tariff
Social	For federal enforcement of Prohibition	For state control of alcohol regulation

QUOTES & CUSTOMS

Second Thoughts In 1919, Franklin Roosevelt said, "Hoover certainly is a wonder, and I wish we could make him President of the United States. There could not be a better one."

Boom and Bust "We in America are nearer to the final triumph over poverty than ever before in the history of any land....Poverty will be banished from this land."

THE LESSONS

1. People tend to "vote their pocketbooks." Prosperous Americans voted Republican. The workers and farmers, who saw prosperity passing them by, voted for a change of party.

2. The religious issue defeated Smith in 1928, but when Kennedy ran a generation later, the issue had less impact.

F.D.R. Pledges a New Deal in 1932

THE CANDIDATES

Franklin D. Roosevelt, the reform governor of New York, was the Democratic choice for President, with **John N. Garner** as his running mate.

Herbert Hoover, the incumbent, was renominated by the Republicans. **Charles Curtis** was selected as the Vice-Presidential candidate.

THE CAMPAIGN

1. Roosevelt, paralyzed by polio as an adult, flew to Chicago to become the first candidate to deliver his acceptance speech in person.
2. F.D.R. campaigned vigorously, pledging "a New Deal for the American people."
3. Before F.D.R. took office, an assassin shot at him in Miami, Florida. The shots missed F.D.R. but killed his companion, Mayor Anton Cermak of Chicago.

THE ISSUES

	Roosevelt (Democrat)	Hoover (Republican)
Foreign	Overshadowed by the Great Depression	Blamed foreign problems for the Depression
Economic	For reform to aid unemployed, provide work for people	Blamed for Great Depression
Social	For repeal of Prohibition, aid to the "forgotten man"	For state control of Prohibition

QUOTES & CUSTOMS

Inaugural Address "The only thing we have to fear is fear itself."

Energy F.D.R.'s good friend Winston Churchill exclaimed, "Meeting him is like opening a bottle of champagne."

Accomplishments With his New Deal, Roosevelt remade the Democratic party and the federal government, creating new agencies and services.

THE LESSONS

1. The American people in 1932 were not happy with Hoover's handling of the Great Depression and voted for F.D.R. without any idea of where the New Deal would take the nation.
2. Much as prosperity had helped place the Republicans in the White House during the 1920's, the Depression helped remove them in 1932.
3. The public agreed to more government control of the economy. This was a great change from the laissez-faire policies of the 1920's.

F.D.R. Continues the New Deal in 1936

THE CANDIDATES

Franklin D. Roosevelt, the incumbent President, was easily renominated and ran with **John Nance Garner,** Democratic representative from Texas and Speaker of the House, who later broke with the President over the court-packing deal and his decision to seek a third term.

Alfred M. Landon, Republican governor from Kansas, ran with **Frank Knox,** Republican newspaper publisher from Illinois.

THE CAMPAIGN

1. Roosevelt and Landon were the first candidates to meet during a campaign since 1912.
2. Roosevelt, in a landslide vote, carried every state but Maine and Vermont.
3. Third-party candidate William Lenke was the first to use an airplane extensively, flying over thirty thousand miles.

THE ISSUES

	Roosevelt (Democrat)	Landon (Republican)
Foreign	For reciprocal trade agreements, international disarmament	For repeal of reciprocal trade agreements, collection of foreign debt
Economic	Pledged to continue the New Deal	Against the New Deal
Social	New Deal supported by unions, farmers, the poor, and blacks	Against the Social Security Act
Personal	Roosevelt's campaign ignored the opposition	Republicans called Roosevelt everything from a dictator to a communist

QUOTES & CUSTOMS

On the Presidency "One of the chief obligations of the Presidency is to think about the future."

A Call "This generation of Americans has a rendezvous with destiny."

Fear of Fire Because of his physical handicap Roosevelt's greatest fear was fire. He never liked being left alone in a room with a fire burning in the fireplace.

Court-Packing Roosevelt's attempt to "pack" the Supreme Court with justices who "would look at modern problems with modern glasses" backfired. Americans did not want to change the traditional structure of the court.

THE LESSONS

1. Public opinion polls do not always accurately predict election outcomes. The Literary Digest poll predicted Landon would win by a landslide in 1936. The poll was skewed in favor of Republicans because it sampled people owning telephones (wealthy) and not the poor.

F.D.R. Wins Third Term in 1940

THE CANDIDATES

Franklin D. Roosevelt, incumbent Democratic President, ran for an unprecedented third term in office. His running mate was **Henry Wallace,** a former Republican who became a Democrat to support Al Smith in 1928 and Roosevelt in 1932.

Wendell L. Willkie, former Democrat turned Republican from Indiana, was a newcomer to national politics. His running mate, **Charles McNary,** Republican senator from Oregon, advised Willkie, "Don't forget, young man, in politics you'll never be in trouble by not saying too much."

THE CAMPAIGN

1. Many felt that Roosevelt's bid for a third term was a serious break with tradition that opened the door to dictatorship.
2. The campaign was overshadowed by the country's growing concern over World War II.

THE ISSUES

	Roosevelt (Democrat)	Willkie (Republican)
Foreign	For a strong, defense; against entry into World War II	For a strong stand against Hitler, a military draft
Economic	For continued New Deal programs	Against inefficient New Deal programs
Social	For "a real job at a living wage" for all wanting to work	For an Equal Rights Amendment

QUOTES & CUSTOMS

Best Defense "The best defense of Britain is the best defense of the United States…We must become the great arsenal of democracy."

On Freedom In his State of the Union address, Roosevelt spoke of the necessity to preserve the four essential freedoms: freedom of speech and expression, freedom to worship God, freedom from want, and freedom from fear.

Travel Roosevelt traveled extensively while President and made twenty-four trips outside the country—more than any other President.

THE LESSONS

1. In the midst of world war, the third-term issue seemed inconsequential to the majority of voters.
2. Willkie failed to offer voters sufficient reason for ousting the incumbent.

F.D.R. Wins Yet Again in 1944

THE CANDIDATES

Franklin D. Roosevelt, incumbent three-term Democratic President, accepted the nomination to run for a fourth term. **Harry S. Truman,** Democratic senator from Missouri, at first declined Roosevelt's offer for the Vice-Presidential nomination but later relented. He became our thirty-third President when F.D.R. died on April 12, 1945.

Thomas E. Dewey, Republican governor from New York, called for new leadership. **John W. Bricker,** Republican governor of Ohio, was unanimously chosen as the Vice-Presidential candidate.

THE CAMPAIGN

1. The 1944 election was the first wartime Presidential contest since 1864.
2. Roosevelt's failing health, rather than foreign or domestic issues, captured the public's attention.
3. The Republican platform called for a two-term limit for the office of the President. This later became the Twenty-second Amendment.

THE ISSUES

	Roosevelt (Democrat)	Dewey (Republican)
Foreign	For postwar world leadership, the creation of a Jewish state in Palestine, a conference of nations	Against isolationism; for a postwar organization of nations and creation of a Jewish state in Palestine
Economic	For equal pay for equal work regardless of sex	For extension of Social Security, unemployment compensation
Social	For an Equal Rights Amendment	Against Roosevelt's "henchmen"; for an Equal Rights Amendment

QUOTES & CUSTOMS

A Fourth Term "All that is within me cries out to go back to my home on the Hudson River…but as a good soldier…I will accept and serve."

On Peace "We can gain no lasting peace if we approach it with suspicion and mistrust—or with fear. We can gain it only if we proceed with the understanding and the confidence and courage which flow from conviction."

Meet the Press Roosevelt held more news conferences than any other President—a record of 998 during his time in office.

Last Written Words "The only limit to our realization of tomorrow will be our doubts of today. Let us move forward with strong and active faith."

THE LESSONS

1. The media played an important part in the campaign. Dewey was photographed standing on two boxes to reach above a lectern, and the public shuddered.
2. During the war, Americans were reluctant to change horses in midstream.

Truman Surprises the Experts in 1948

THE CANDIDATES

Harry S. Truman, the Democratic incumbent succeeded Roosevelt in 1945, therefore serving almost all of Roosevelt's fourth term. **Alben W. Barkley,** Kentucky senator, roused the convention with his fiery keynote address.

Thomas E. Dewey, Republican governor of New York, lost this campaign by trying to stay above it. **Earl Warren,** governor of California, would agree to be on the ticket only after being guaranteed a major policy-making role.

THE CAMPAIGN

1. Southern conservatives left the Democratic party in droves and supported Strom Thurmond of the States' Rights party. Thurmond won four Southern states.
2. Most of the media predicted a Dewey victory. In 1946 the Republicans had won control of Congress, and the country seemed to be turning away from the Roosevelt/ Truman era.
3. Neither the popular nor the electoral vote turned out to be close; Truman won decisively.

THE ISSUES

	Truman (Democrat)	Dewey (Republican)
Foreign	For foreign aid, NATO, containment of communism	Stressed the pursuit of subversives as a way of fighting the Cold War
Economic	Blamed Congress for obstructing passage of housing legislation and a minimum wage	Believed that housing is best financed by private enterprise
Social	For civil rights legislation	For states' rights, but favored abolition of both the poll tax and military segregation

QUOTES & CUSTOMS

Surprise! "When they told me yesterday what had happened [Roosevelt's death], I felt like the moon, the stars, and all the planets had fallen on me."

On His Presidency "Some of the Presidents were great, and some of them weren't. I can say that because I wasn't one of the great Presidents; but I had a good time trying to be one."

Savior Winston Churchill, Britain's Prime Minister during the war, praised Truman for the Marshall Plan saying, "You, more than any other man, have saved Western civilization."

THE LESSONS

1. Truman's "whistlestop" tour by train allowed him to travel thousands of miles and to make hundreds of speeches. His sincerity won the crowds, who shouted, "Give 'em hell, Harry!"
2. The public opinion polls and experts are not always right.

Eisenhower Wins for Republicans in 1952

THE CANDIDATES

Dwight D. Eisenhower, the commander of NATO forces in Europe, was a war hero in World War II. He was recruited by both parties but was nominated on the first ballot at the Republican convention. Vice-Presidential candidate **Richard M. Nixon,** senator from California, was famous for his investigation of Alger Hiss.

Adlai E. Stevenson, governor of Illinois, was hand-picked by Truman for the Democratic nomination but was little known outside Illinois. **John J. Sparkman,** Democratic senator from Alabama, was a compromise candidate for Vice-President.

THE CAMPAIGN

1. After the first primary, President Truman announced he would not run.
2. Anti-communism was the chief issue in the campaign.
3. The size of Eisenhower's landslide surprised the pollsters; he won by 6.5 million popular votes.

THE ISSUES

	Eisenhower (Republican)	Stevenson (Democrat)
Foreign	For military victory in Korean War; Eisenhower promised to go to Korea	Promised "peace with honor" which would be achieved by support for a strengthened U.N.
Economic	The platform charged that the New and Fair Deals had led to inflation	For extension of Social Security, closing of tax loopholes
Social	Accused Democrats of dragging feet in prosecuting corruption and communists	Defended the Bill of Rights against McCarthyites

QUOTES & CUSTOMS

War and Peace "The people who know war, those who have experienced it, I believe are the most earnest advocates of peace in the world."

Interstate Highways Eisenhower supported a huge highway construction program including the interstate highway system.

THE LESSONS

1. The election of 1952 showed that the image of the candidate is more important than his political party.
2. Americans tend to vote for change after one political party has dominated the Presidency for a long time.

Eisenhower Enjoys a Landslide in 1956

THE CANDIDATES

Dwight D. Eisenhower, the Republican incumbent, was an extremely popular President at a relatively prosperous time. **Richard M. Nixon,** Eisenhower's Vice-President, was labeled the New Nixon when he toned down his attacks on Democratic leaders.

Adlai E. Stevenson, the Democrat trying again to defeat Eisenhower, was a good speaker with an excellent sense of humor. **Estes Kefauver,** Democratic senator from Tennessee, won the Vice-Presidential nomination.

THE CAMPAIGN

1. In a surprise move, Stevenson asked the convention to name his running mate.
2. Eisenhower did less campaigning in 1956, mainly because of his health; he suffered a heart attack in 1955 and underwent an operation for ileitis in June of 1956.
3. Eisenhower's landslide was the greatest since Roosevelt defeated Landon in 1936. However, Republicans failed to win the majority in either the House or the Senate.

THE ISSUES

	Eisenhower (Republican)	Stevenson (Democrat)
Foreign	For Israeli nation, the Eisenhower Doctrine	Against the draft, nuclear testing
Economic	For reduction of government spending outside of defense, balanced budget	Blamed the Republicans for allowing big business to dominate the economy; for tax cuts for lower-income people
Social	Supported the Supreme Court decision in *Brown* v. *Board of Education of Topeka*	For states' as well as civil rights

QUOTES & CUSTOMS

Camp David Eisenhower changed the name of F.D.R.'s Maryland retreat from Shangri-la to Camp David, saying that Shangri-la was "just a little too fancy for a Kansas farm boy."

Integration After the Brown v. Board of Education of Topeka decision, Eisenhower sent federal troops to Arkansas to protect black students in Little Rock in 1957.

Military Influence "We must guard against the acquisition of unwarranted influence…by the military-industrial complex."

THE LESSONS

1. The election of 1956 showed that the Solid South could no longer be depended upon by the Democrats.
2. A very popular incumbent may take the high ground during a campaign.

Kennedy Pursues a New Frontier in 1960

THE CANDIDATES

John F. Kennedy, Democratic senator from Massachusetts. **Lyndon B. Johnson,** a surprise choice because of his own Presidential aspirations, balanced the ticket to give it Southern appeal.

Richard M. Nixon, Republican Vice-President, was not completely supported by Eisenhower. **Henry Cabot Lodge, Jr.,** popular United Nations ambassador, was his running mate.

THE CAMPAIGN

1. The focus of the campaign was a series of televised debates. Kennedy's calm, confident manner on television gained supporters; Nixon seemed tentative and weary.
2. Voter turnout was the largest ever at that time, and the vote was so close that the outcome was not clear until the following day.
3. Republicans suspected vote fraud, particularly in Texas and Chicago, but Nixon refused to pursue an investigation.

THE ISSUES

	Kennedy (Democrat)	Nixon (Republican)
Foreign	For strong defense—warned of "missile gap"	Claimed to be strong on Russia, citing the Kitchen Debates with Khrushchev
Economic	For aid to combat recession	Denied recession
Social	For strong civil rights, increased Social Security	For civil rights but wanted Southern support
Personal	Kennedy's Catholicism was the object of much bigotry, but both candidates tried to avoid the issue	Nixon was often viewed as an opportunist by the press

QUOTES & CUSTOMS

Inaugural Address "And so, my fellow Americans: ask not what your country can do for you—ask what you can do for your country."

Peace Corps In March 1961, the Peace Corps was started to enlist "the services of all those with the desire and capacity to help foreign lands meet their urgent needs for trained personnel."

Civil Rights "This nation…will not be fully free until all its citizens are free."

Assassination After Kennedy was killed in November 1963, Johnson addressed Congress, saying, "All I have I would have given gladly not to be standing here today."

THE LESSONS

1. The election of 1960 proved that the image projected by a candidate on television is vital to his or her election chances.
2. Election-day polls showed that religion still played a serious role in the campaign results despite both candidates' attempts to downplay the issue.

Johnson Builds a Great Society in 1964

THE CANDIDATES

Lyndon B. Johnson, the incumbent Democratic President, had been an effective advocate of Kennedy's programs with his skillful direction of Congress. **Hubert H. Humphrey,** Democratic senator from Minnesota, represented the liberal wing of the Democratic party.

Barry Goldwater, Republican senator from Arizona, revived the conservative wing of the Republican party. **William E. Miller,** a New York congressman, was not well-known, and his conservative views did little to balance the Republican ticket.

THE CAMPAIGN

1. Goldwater's philosophy and comments renewed interest in conservative politics.
2. Johnson won in a landslide with 61 percent of the total vote cast. In addition, Democrats increased their majorities in Congress.

THE ISSUES

	Johnson (Democrat)	Goldwater (Republican)
Foreign	For restraint in Vietnam War	Against disarmament; for military decisions to use nuclear weapons
Economic	Declared a War on Poverty	For massive cuts in social spending; against "big government"
Social	For strong Civil Rights Act	Believed that civil rights were subject to states' rights

QUOTES & CUSTOMS

Being President "Ain't near as bad as being Vice-President. Not being able to do anything will wear you down sooner than hard work."

On Vietnam "We are not about to send American boys nine to ten thousand miles away from home to do what Asian boys ought to be doing for themselves."

Great Society Johnson led Congress to approve aid to education, Medicare, strong civil-rights bills, and new cabinet departments—HUD and Transportation.

THE LESSONS

1. Party divisions which are aggravated in the national convention will doom a national election.
2. Johnson, in 1968, followed the unwritten rule that no "accidental" President has ever been twice elected to the Presidency.

Nixon Wins the White House in 1968

THE CANDIDATES

Richard M. Nixon, former Republican Vice-President under Eisenhower, made a comeback after losing elections in 1960 and 1962. **Spiro T. Agnew,** Republican governor of Maryland was chosen to win votes in the South.

Hubert H. Humphrey, Johnson's Vice-President, was the Democratic choice for President. **Edmund S. Muskie,** Democratic senator from Maine, was the Vice-Presidential candidate.

George C. Wallace, former governor of Alabama, ran as the strongest third-party candidate in forty-four years for the American Independent party.

THE CAMPAIGN

1. President Johnson sacrificed his political career to end the war in Vietnam when he refused to run again.
2. When the front-runner candidate, Bobby Kennedy, was assassinated, the Democratic party was bitterly divided.
3. Not since 1800, when Jefferson defeated Adams, had a former (Nixon) and an incumbent (Humphrey) Vice-President run against each other.

THE ISSUES

	Nixon (Republican)	Humphrey (Democrat)
Foreign	For "just peace" in Vietnam	Against the Vietnam War
Economic	For less governmental interference	For Great Society programs
Social	For return to law and order	For advances in civil rights and education
Personal	Humphrey called Nixon "Richard the Chickenhearted" for avoiding a debate I	Nixon blamed Humphrey for the policies of the Johnson administration

QUOTES & CUSTOMS

Salary A week before Nixon's inauguration, Congress doubled the Presidential salary from $100,000 to $200,000.

Moon Walk Nixon telephoned the first astronauts on the moon, saying, "For one priceless moment in the whole history of man all the people on this earth are truly one—one in their pride in what you have done, and one in our prayers that you will return safely to Earth."

Open Door Sixty million Americans watched Nixon's unprecedented visit to mainland China in televised ceremonies.

THE LESSONS

1. Nixon was only the fourth Vice-President in our history to be elected President. Eight others became President upon the death of their predecessors.
2. George Wallace's success in getting on all fifty ballots showed that the obstacles to third-party candidates were not as large as previously thought.

Nixon Wins but Scandal Follows in 1972

THE CANDIDATES

Richard M. Nixon, the Republican incumbent, despite great success with foreign policy, was later forced to resign because of the Watergate scandal. **Spiro T. Agnew,** Nixon's Vice-President, was forced to resign in 1973 because of a bribery scandal.

George S. McGovern, Democratic senator from South Dakota, received support from young voters for his anti-Vietnam stance. **R. Sargent Shriver,** former Ambassador to France, replaced Senator Thomas Eagleton as McGovern's Vice-Presidential candidate.

THE CAMPAIGN

1. Newspapers carried stories during the campaign that linked the Watergate break-in to the White House. Official denials and efforts to end the Vietnam War diverted public attention.

2. Senator Eagleton was forced off the Democratic ticket when it was disclosed that he had been hospitalized for mental depression on several occasions in the past.

THE ISSUES

	Nixon (Republican)	McGovern (Democrat)
Foreign	For U.S. cooperation with China and U.S.S.R.; waged an unpopular war in Vietnam	Against war in Vietnam
Economic	For free enterprise; against guaranteed income	Promised $1000 to every poverty-stricken family; for tax reform
Social	Against busing, gun control	For busing, racial integration

QUOTES & CUSTOMS

On Watergate "I was wrong in not acting more decisively and more forthrightly in dealing with Watergate, particularly when it reached the stage of judicial proceedings and grew from a political scandal into a national tragedy."

Resignation When impeachment and conviction became all but certain, Nixon resigned on August 9, 1974, becoming the only President in history to do so.

THE LESSONS

1. The election of 1972, like 1964, showed that a candidate whose ideas are perceived to be outside the mainstream will not be successful.

2. Unethical or criminal actions are only aggravated by attempts to cover them up.

Carter Leads the South to Victory in 1976

THE CANDIDATES

James E. Carter, former Democratic governor of Georgia, claimed his "outsider" status would be helpful in corrupt Washington. **Walter F. Mondale,** Democratic senator from Minnesota, balanced the ticket because of his Northern home state and his liberal views.

Gerald R. Ford, the first person to occupy the Presidency and the Vice-Presidency without being elected to either office, never really escaped Nixon's shadow. **Robert Dole,** Republican senator from Kansas, was chosen as the Vice-Presidential candidate.

THE CAMPAIGN

1. Carter began his campaign saying, "My name is Jimmy Carter, and I'm running for President."

2. Both candidates made serious mistakes. During a televised debate, Ford asserted that there was no Soviet domination of Eastern Europe; Carter had to apologize for an interview in a magazine.

THE ISSUES

	Carter (Democrat)	Ford (Republican)
Foreign	Strong concern for human rights	Continued Nixon/Kissinger policy
Economic	For Full employment as solution to the country's troubled economy; Carter was generally a fiscal conservative	Inflation, unemployment, and recession forced cuts in spending and taxes; against foreign energy imports
Social	For equal rights	For traditional values; against abortion, gun control

QUOTES & CUSTOMS

Outsider "I have been accused of being an outsider. I plead guilty. Unfortunately, the vast majority of Americans are also outsiders."

With the People To emphasize his ties with the people, Carter walked the inaugural parade route from the Capitol to the White House, the first ever to do so.

THE LESSONS

1. Early campaigning establishes name recognition in the small, early primary states like Iowa and New Hampshire.

2. A Southern Democrat may be able to unite Southern conservative states with Northern liberal states for a Democratic victory.

Reagan Overturns an Incumbent in 1980

THE CANDIDATES

Ronald W. Reagan, the former governor of California, won the Republican nomination in his second formal attempt at the White House. **George Bush,** office-holder in several Republican administrations, was picked by Reagan for Vice-President.

James E. Carter, the incumbent Democratic President, suffered from high inflation at home and the Iranian hostage crisis abroad. **Walter Mondale,** Carter's Vice-President, was one of the few speakers at the Democratic Convention to praise his boss's record.

THE CAMPAIGN

1. Carter fought challenges from Edward Kennedy and John Anderson's third-party candidacy before winning the nomination.
2. Carter's defeat was the worst for an incumbent President since Hoover's loss to Roosevelt in 1932.
3. Reagan's victory was accompanied by the first Republican majority in the Senate since 1954.

THE ISSUES

	Reagan (Republican)	Carter (Democrat)
Foreign	For strong commitments to allies; against communism	Difficulty with the hostage crisis; used embargoes to enforce human rights
Economic	Promised to cut taxes, increase defense	Agreed to wage and price controls spending, and balance the budget
Social	For traditional values, school prayer; against abortion	For equal rights for women and minorities

QUOTES & CUSTOMS

Economics "I'm told I can't use the word 'depression.' Well, I'll tell you the definition. A recession is when your neighbor loses his job, and a depression is when you lose your job. Recovery is when Jimmy Carter loses his!"

On Government Waste "There's enough fat in the government in Washington that if it was rendered and made into soap, it would wash the world."

THE LESSONS

1. The election of 1980 showed the importance of a healthy economy for an incumbent President to win reelection.
2. An anti-candidate vote may be as important as, or more important than, a pro-candidate vote.

Reagan Wins Another Landslide in 1984

THE CANDIDATES

Ronald W. Reagan, the Republican incumbent, faced the election with ideal conditions. **George Bush,** Reagan's Vice-President, was criticized for having too little influence in the administration.

Walter F. Mondale, former Vice-President under Carter, was the Democratic candidate. **Geraldine Ferraro,** Democratic congresswoman from New York, was the first woman on a major Presidential ticket.

THE CAMPAIGN

1. Reagan and Mondale debated the issues on television. Reagan's mistakes in the first debate were covered with more humor and fewer statistics in the second debate.
2. Reagan won in a tremendous landslide; his margin of victory was more than 17 million votes. He won the electoral vote 525 to 13.

THE ISSUES

	Reagan (Republican)	Mondale (Democrat)
Foreign	For arms control, strong stance against communism	Against hard-line approach to communism
Economic	For supply-side economics, cutbacks in social spending; against cuts in military spending	Against deficit; for higher taxes
Social	For traditional values; against affirmative action	For Equal Rights Amendment, affirmative action

QUOTES & CUSTOMS

Age At seventy-three, Reagan was the oldest candidate to campaign. He quipped, "I'm afraid the age factor may play a part in this election. Our opponent's ideas are too old." He also said, "I will not make age an issue of this campaign. I'm not going to exploit for political purposes my opponent's youth and inexperience."

Religion "The truth is, politics and morality are inseparable, and as morality's foundation is religion, religion and politics are necessarily related. We need religion for a guide."

THE LESSONS

1. The election of 1984 showed that a popular incumbent and a strong economy is a winning combination.
2. A candidate running on the issue of higher taxes will not be popular.

Bush Continues Republican Leadership in 1988

THE CANDIDATES

George H. W. Bush, the incumbent Vice-President, represented traditional Republican views. **J. Danforth Quayle** was selected as Bush's running mate for his strength in valuable Midwestern states.

Michael S. Dukakis, Democratic governor of Massachusetts, called for party unity and positioned himself as a centrist. **Lloyd Bentsen,** Democratic senator of Texas, was chosen as his running mate.

THE CAMPAIGN

1. Bush accused Dukakis of being "a liberal" who was out of touch with the American people. He implied Dukakis would raise taxes if elected.
2. Bush overcame a significant Dukakis pre-election lead in the polls to win handily.

THE ISSUES

	Bush (Republican)	Dukakis (Democrat)
Foreign	For Reagan's arms control initiatives, development of SDI, aid to Contras, U.S. naval presence in the Persian Gulf, constructive engagement in dealing with South Africa	For Reagan's arms control initiatives, research on SDI, partnerships rather than unilateral movement in the Gulf, strong sanctions against South Africa
Economic	For $2 billion child care program, tax-free college savings bonds; against protectionism, higher taxes	For Congress' child care bill, a raise in minimum wage, $500 million regional economic development plan
Social	For current drug enforcement program plus death penalty for large-scale drug dealers; against abortion	For $1 billion for AIDS research, current free-choice abortion policy; against aid to drug-dealing governments

QUOTES & CUSTOMS

Bush Plans Action "We have earned our optimism, we have a right to our confidence, and we have much to do."

Bush on Taxes "Read my lips. No new taxes!"

THE LESSONS

1. The election emphasized that money is extremely important to sustain a Presidential candidate during the prolonged primary season. Bush's campaign cost more than $75 million.
2. Taxes continue to be an important but slippery issue to voters and candidates. The country will not vote for a candidate supporting an obvious tax hike.

Clinton Taps Thirst for Change in 1992

THE CANDIDATES

Bill Clinton, Democratic governor of Arkansas, focused his campaign on the nation's weak economy. **Al Gore,** senator of Tennessee, was Clinton's running mate.

George Bush enjoyed popularity following the Persian Gulf War in 1991. But his popularity plummeted when a recession gripped the nation. **Dan Quayle** was his running mate again.

THE CAMPAIGN

1. Bush remained relatively quiet until the Republican convention in August.
2. Clinton and Gore, on the other hand, conducted bus tours to various states.
3. H. Ross Perot, a Texas businessman, ran for president as the candidate of the Reform Party.

THE ISSUES

	Clinton (Democrat)	Bush (Republican)
Foreign	For making the nation internationally competitive, a nuclear test ban treaty	For normal trade status for China, reducing dependence on foreign oil by off-shore drilling in Alaska, defusing Hussein (Iraq)
Economic	For reform of health care costs, balancing the budget deficit, expanding industries and jobs, a moratorium on building nuclear power plants; against drilling for oil off the Alaskan coast	For building 150 new nuclear reactors by the year 2030, tax credits for first-time home buyers, balancing the budget; against further raising standards for automobile air pollution.
Social	For providing health care for all Americans, social justice, war on drugs and crime, protecting the environment, women's right to choice (abortion), college loans	For welfare reform, "family values," fighting crime and drugs, capital punishment; against abortion

QUOTES & CUSTOMS

Clinton on Bush "He took the richest country in the world and brought it down. We took one of the poorest states and lifted it up."

Bush on the Recession "I simply cannot be satisfied until every American who wants a job has one."

THE LESSONS

1. Candidates not only win votes for their vision and promises but also win "protest votes" against the incumbent.
2. The failure of a President to lead the nation out of a recession can hurt his chances of reelection.
3. Elections hinge in large part on foreign and domestic conditions just before voting time: peace and prosperity win votes.

THE CANDIDATES

Bill Clinton, incumbent President, proposed an agenda that seemed more Republican than Democratic, but he opposed extremely conservative measures. Vice President **Al Gore** was Clinton's running mate.

Bob Dole, U.S. Senator from Kansas, served for 35 years on Capitol Hill. **Jack Kemp**—a former football star, congressman from New York, and cabinet member—was Dole's running mate.

THE CAMPAIGN

1. Clinton demonstrated his brilliance as a campaigner and convinced many Americans that the Republicans threatened many important programs.
2. Dole resigned his Senate seat in order to campaign full time but still trailed Clinton throughout the race.

THE ISSUES

	Clinton (Democrat)	Dole (Republican)
Foreign	For expanding NATO, negotiating Middle East peace, supporting peacekeeping efforts in Bosnia	For an active U.S. role; new missile defense system
Economic	For targeted tax cuts and balancing the federal budget; reduction in income taxes	For a constitutional amendment to balance the budget
Social	For health insurance for children, tax incentives to increase college attendance, hiring 100,000 police officers, abortion rights, ban on assault weapons	For building more prisons; appointing judges who are "tough on crime"; against abortion rights, affirmative action, and most gun-control measures

QUOTES AND CUSTOMS

Clinton's Aim Clinton hoped that his presidency would be viewed as a "bridge to the twenty-first century."

Reinventing Government Having cut the federal payroll by 250,000 jobs, Clinton and Gore renewed their pledge to streamline government bureaucracy.

THE LESSONS

1. Although Clinton and Gore were re-elected, voters also elected a Republican Congress. This situation required bipartisan cooperation between the President and Congress.
2. The economy is a major factor in elections. Although Clinton was the target of Senate probes, the strength of the economy—plus his apparent willingness to learn from his mistakes—led to his reelection.

THE CANDIDATES

George W. Bush, the governor of Texas and son of former President Bush, wanted to privatize Social Security and cut income tax rates. **Dick Cheney,** Secretary of Defense under the former President Bush, was George W. Bush's running mate.

Patrick J. Buchanan, a conservative journalist, ran as the nominee of the Reform Party.

Al Gore, the incumbent Vice-President, played a major role in policymaking decisions during the Clinton administration. **U.S. Senator Joe Lieberman** was the first Jew ever nominated for the vice presidency by a major party.

Ralph Nader, a consumer advocate, ran as the candidate of the Green Party.

THE CAMPAIGN

1. By the time of the election, the race was too close to call.
2. For five weeks after Election Day, the winner was in doubt. In the end, the U.S. Supreme Court stopped the ballot recounts, giving the election to Bush.

THE ISSUES

	Bush (Republican)	Gore (Democrat)
Foreign	For reducing U.S. peacekeeping missions; new missile defense system	For expanding NATO; supports U.S. peace keeping roles
Economic	For tax cuts; allowing workers to place their Social Security taxes into individual accounts for the poor and middle class	For reducing national debt; using the budget surplus to strengthen Social Security; tax cuts
Social	For capital punishment; reforming Medicare; against abortion rights, affirmative action, and most gun-control measures	For abortion rights, national handgun registration; addition of a prescription drug benefit to Medicare

QUOTES & CUSTOMS

Bush on Government He promised "compassionate conservatism."

Gore on the Recount "What is at stake is the integrity of our democracy."

THE LESSONS

1. Every vote counts. With the election so close, many Americans who had not voted wished that they had.
2. Image is an important factor in elections. Many Americans said they voted based on which candidate they found more likable.
3. Voting procedures need to be improved.

THE CANDIDATES

George W. Bush, incumbent president, ran on the Republican ticket. During his first term, he had initiated a war on terrorism, which included the invasions of Afghanistan and Iraq. Vice President **Richard Cheney** was Bush's running mate.

John F. Kerry, a U.S. senator from Massachusetts, was the Democratic challenger. Kerry was a strong environmentalist. He also opposed tax cuts for the wealthy. **John Edwards,** a U.S. senator from North Carolina, was Kerry's running mate.

THE CAMPAIGN

1. Moral issues, especially abortion and gay marriages, played a crucial role in the election.

2. Controversies involving Bush's and Kerry's military records surfaced during the campaign.

3. High voter turnout indicted that Americans were deeply concerned about the election's outcome.

4. Other candidates in the race included David Cobb of the Green Party; Ralph Nader an independent; Michael Badnarik of the United States Libertarian Party; and Michael Perontka of the Constitution Party.

THE ISSUES

	Bush (Republican)	Kerry (Democrat)
Foreign	For the elimination of terrorism using any means necessary, including pre-emptive war	Against using force except as a last resort, after all other avenues have been exhausted
Economic	For permanent tax cuts	For elimination of tax breaks for the wealthy; against tax cuts for companies outsourcing jobs
Social	For looser environmental controls, Medical Savings Accounts, privatization of Social Security; against abortion rights, gay marriages	For environmental protection, comprehensive health care, against privatizing Social Security, for abortion rights, for civil liberties for all (including gays and lesbians)

QUOTES AND CUSTOMS

Bush on Winning "I earned capital in this campaign, political capital, and now I intend to spend it."

Kerry on Conceding "The outcome should be decided by voters, not a protracted legal process."

THE LESSONS

1. Foreign and domestic policy may be less important to many Americans than "moral" issues.

2. Voting procedures—especially Direct Recording Electronic Systems—may not be accurate or reliable.

3. The Internet has become a factor in elections. It provides information about the candidates and an alternative means of fund raising.

The 2000 Presidential Campaign

THE CAMPAIGN BEGINS

The United States moved into its eighth year of economic growth as the 2000 presidential campaign began. The strong economy appeared to give the Democrats—the party that held the White House during much of the 1990s—a leg up in the campaign. Most Americans applauded President Bill Clinton's economic policies. Many citizens, however, believed that Clinton failed to provide moral leadership. Clinton spent much of his second term mired in a scandal that led to his impeachment. A Fall 1999 poll showed that a majority of Americans were "just plain tired" of him. Republicans believed Americans wanted a change in Washington despite the good economic times. Thus, the GOP eagerly looked to regain the White House.

The Candidates Texas governor George W. Bush emerged as the leading Republican candidate. Vice President Al Gore was the Democratic frontrunner. Both men came from prestigious political families. Bush's father, George Herbert Walker Bush, was the nation's president from 1989 to 1993. Similarly, Al Gore, Sr., a Tennessee Democrat, served in both houses of Congress.

Despite these similarities, the two candidates followed different paths in politics. After a brief stint as a journalist, Gore ran for Congress in 1976. He won that race and served eight years in the U. S. House before winning a seat in the U.S. Senate. In Congress, Gore earned a reputation as a moderate and an expert on nuclear arms control and the environment. Gore ran unsuccessfully for the Democratic presidential nomination in 1988. In 1992, Gore was elected vice president on the ticket headed by Clinton.

Bush, on the other hand, was a relative newcomer to politics. He spent much of his career engaged in various business ventures. He had been in the oil exploration business and later became co-owner of the Texas Rangers baseball team. In 1978, he narrowly lost an election for the U.S. House of Representatives from a district in western Texas. His second bid for elective office proved more successful, as he won election as Texas governor in 1994. Then he won reelection in 1998 by a large majority. As governor, Bush won praise for his ability to work with Democrats and build coalitions. When his name emerged among potential presidential candidates, many Republican Party leaders lined up to support him.

The Primaries Despite each candidate's stature, however, neither one enjoyed a clear path to their party's nomination. The Republican field was crowded with candidates, but Bush was still heavily favored. He had a large campaign war chest and widespread support from party leaders. Nevertheless, the Bush campaign suffered a shocking early setback at the hands of Arizona senator John McCain. McCain was a Vietnam War hero who had made campaign finance reform his main issue. In February 2000, he defeated Bush by nearly 20 points in the New Hampshire primary.

Bush vowed to overcome this defeat. Eventually he did. The McCain campaign could not maintain its drive. By spring, Governor Bush had claimed enough primary victories to cinch the Republican nomination.

On the Democratic side, Al Gore faced a primary challenge from former U. S. Senator and one-time professional basketball player Bill Bradley. Bradley ran as a liberal alternative to the Vice President. He offered proposals to reduce poverty and provide near universal health-care coverage. Bradley raised a considerable amount of money and nearly beat Gore in the New Hampshire primary. The Bradley campaign soon fizzled, however, and Gore won the Democratic nomination.

While Bush and Gore were sewing up the major party nominations, two other candidates were also moving ahead. Consumer advocate Ralph Nader was running on the Green Party ticket. He ran on a progressive platform that focused on protecting the environment, providing universal health care, and fostering economic fairness. He also wanted campaign finance reform and stronger regulation of corporations. Many Democrats feared that Nader's campaign might draw support from liberals who might otherwise vote for Gore.

Meanwhile, conservative journalist Pat Buchanan was winning the Reform Party nomination. Ross Perot, the party's founder, decided not to make a third run for the presidency. Buchanan and another candidate named John Hagelin fought for control of the party, but Buchanan won the nomination. Many Republicans feared that Buchanan might take conservative votes away from Bush.

A SEE-SAW BATTLE

As the presidential race went into full swing, the spotlight remained on the two major candidates. Both Bush and Gore emphasized the themes of their campaigns. Touting his experience at the highest levels of government, Gore argued that he was better prepared than Bush to keep the nation's economy booming. "I want to keep our prosperity going, and I know how to do it," he declared. Gore also promised voters greater "moral leadership" in the oval office and promised to fight hard for middle class families.

Meanwhile, Bush called himself a "compassionate conservative." As such, he promised to support traditional Republican priorities, such as cutting taxes, limiting government, and increasing individual responsibility. Meanwhile, he also showed concern for underprivileged Americans. "I'm running because I want our party to match a conservative mind with a compassionate heart," he said.

The Main Issues On a few key issues, the candidates had important differences. For example, Bush proposed a $1.3 trillion cut in income tax rates over the next 10 years. Such a cut would reduce the nation's budget surplus, which was projected to reach about $2 trillion by 2010. Bush claimed that such a large tax break would encourage greater spending and investment, stimulating faster economic growth. Democrats argued, however, that most of this $1.3 trillion would go to wealthy households. Accordingly, Gore called for a smaller tax cut—about $480 billion—aimed mainly at lower and middle-class Americans.

Second, both candidates offered different plans to strengthen Social Security—the federal program to provide financial security for senior citizens. Many people feared the program would face a financial crisis when the nation's large baby boom population began to retire early in the 21st century. Bush called for allowing workers to invest some of their Social Security taxes in the stock market. He hoped that such investments would increase in value over time. As these investments would grow, they would reduce the government's financial burden for future payments. By contrast, Gore sought to help Social Security by paying off the national debt, which would eliminate interest payments made by the government. He proposed devoting the money saved on these interest payments—around $200 billion annually—to the Social Security fund.

Third, the candidates took different positions on health care insurance. Perhaps the most important problem was that 43 million Americans were uninsured and millions of others could not afford full coverage. Bush called for giving uninsured families a $2,000 tax credit to purchase insurance. Gore, however, promised to provide every child with health insurance. He also offered expanded health coverage for poor and middle-class families.

A Seeming Stalemate By Labor Day, polls showed the race to be a dead heat, and the campaign remained close through Election Day. One reason that neither candidate could pull away was that each battled unfavorable images on the campaign trail. On one hand, many people saw Gore as stiff and colorless. Others questioned his truthfulness and linked him to Clinton's scandals. On the other hand, many thought Bush lacked the intellect and drive to lead the nation. As Election Day approached, most polls showed Bush holding a slight lead over Gore. Americans prepared for what many observers insisted would be the most suspenseful presidential election in decades. No one, however, expected what actually happened.

THE CLOSEST ELECTION IN MEMORY

On the eve of the election on November 7, 2000, polls showed that the race would be one of the tightest ever. The election proved even closer than expected, and neither Bush nor Gore could claim immediate victory. For more than a month after Election Day, Americans faced the drama and uncertainty of what one magazine called "The Wildest Election in History."

Election Night Confusion As election night unfolded, Al Gore appeared to take the lead. The television networks declared Gore the winner in Florida, Pennsylvania, and Michigan. These three states were rich in electoral votes, which many people believed would decide the election. Then, in a stunning turn of events, the networks took back their prediction of a Gore victory in Florida. They declared the state "too close to call."

As midnight passed, the race remained neck and neck. It became clear that whoever won Florida would gain the necessary 270 electoral votes to win the election. Around 2 A.M., the networks predicted Bush the winner of Florida— and thus the presidency. Gore called the Texas governor to congratulate him. Gore then headed off to deliver his concession speech.

The chaotic night took yet another twist, however. As the final votes in Florida rolled in, Bush's lead shrank. The state again became too close to call. In what was a first in American history, the vice president called Bush again and took back his concession. When the sun rose the next day, Gore held a slim lead—two-tenths of one percent—in the popular vote. Meanwhile, all eyes turned to Florida, as Bush's razor-thin lead there triggered an automatic recount to determine the final winner of the state—and the presidency.

A Battle Rages in Florida In the weeks following the election, scores of campaign officials traveled to Florida to secure the election for their candidate. The recount of the state's ballots gave Bush a 300-vote lead, but the battle did not end there.

In the days after the election, the public learned of voting irregularities in several Florida counties. Hundreds of African Americans complained of voting-rights violations. For example, some claimed their names were purged from voting rolls after being incorrectly identified as convicted felons. Others said that old voting equipment in predominantly black precincts didn't count votes properly. These problems hurt Gore because more than 90 percent of African-American voters supported him.

Meanwhile, voters in Palm Beach County—another heavily Democratic area—complained that a confusing ballot design caused them to cast their ballots incorrectly. Some spoiled their ballots by punching more than one hole on the ballot. Others said they accidentally punched for the wrong candidate. There were more than 19,000 spoiled ballots in this county alone.

Prompted by these problems, the Gore campaign called for a manual, or hand, recount in four predominantly Democratic counties in Florida. The Bush campaign opposed the recounts, arguing that it opened the door to political mischief. On November 11, the Bush campaign sued to stop the recounts. Over the next month, the two sides battled in the courts over whether the hand counts should proceed.

The legal fight ultimately reached the Supreme Court. Many observers were surprised that the Court decided to hear the case. Many people thought the Court would want to avoid stepping into a presidential election. On December 12, a deeply divided Court ruled 5 to 4 to stop the hand recounts. The majority argued that because the counting process lacked uniform standards and did not include all ballots, it violated the equal protection of all voters. The next night, Gore and Bush made nationally televised speeches. First, Gore conceded the election. Then Bush addressed the country as the new president-elect. Both men called for Americans to move beyond the divisiveness of the election just past and focus on working together for the nation's future. Five weeks after Americans cast their ballots, one of the strangest and most divisive elections in U.S. history had ended.

The Aftermath of the Election In the wake of such a close and contentious election, several issues arose. The most immediate issue was how effectively Bush could govern. With no clear mandate and questions about the legitimacy of his victory, observers wondered whether the new president could lead the nation. Furthermore, the 2000 elections produced a 50-50 Republican-Democratic split in the Senate and a narrow 9-seat Republican majority in the House of Representatives. Such a scenario had journalists across the nation predicting legislative gridlock for the immediate future.

Adding to the potential for gridlock was the bitterness felt by Democrats about Gore's defeat. Many were frustrated by the fact that Gore won the popular vote but not the presidency. Some argued the U.S. Supreme Court decision prevented Americans from ever knowing which candidate truly received the most votes in Florida. In addition, it appeared that Democratic fears about Nader's candidacy were well founded. Nader received nearly 100,000 votes in Florida, easily enough for Gore to have carried the state. All of this made Democrats less willing to accept Bush's leadership.

Other issues that emerged concerned the roles of the media and the Supreme Court in the election. For their part, television executives vowed to reexamine their prediction methods, which had contributed to much of the chaos on election night. "We don't just have egg on our face," said one anchorman about the twice-blown calls in Florida. "We have an omelet." Meanwhile, some

Americans believed the Supreme Court's decision to take part in the election and determine the outcome would tarnish the Court's reputation for fairness.

As for the nation at large, the 2000 election prompted a reexamination of the entire election process. The turmoil in Florida highlighted troubling aspects of the nation's voting system. From out-of-date machines to confusing ballots, there were numerous examples of the system's imperfections. The fact that the candidate that won the popular vote lost the presidency rekindled the debate over the Electoral College. Critics of the system argued that it undermined majority rule. By contrast, defenders of the Electoral College insisted that it strengthened democracy by forcing candidates to pay attention to voters in more states than they would otherwise. What most people seemed to agree on, however, was that the nation would not soon forget its first presidential election of the 21st century.

QUESTIONS

1. Why were the Republicans optimistic about their chances in the 2000 presidential election?

2. How were the backgrounds of Vice President Al Gore and Governor George W. Bush similar? How were they different?

3. What attributes might a long-time member of Congress bring to the presidency? What attributes might a political outsider bring?

4. How might a competitive primary race be an advantage to a presidential candidate headed for the general election? How might it be a disadvantage?

5. What were three key issues in the 2000 election and what positions did the major candidates take on them?

6. How did television help to create confusion on election night?

7. Why might an evenly split Congress lead to legislative gridlock in Washington?

8. Do you think the Electoral College should remain a part of the election process? Explain.

9. There was much talk about "moral leadership" during the election of 2000. Do you think it is important for the president to provide moral leadership? Why or Why not?

10. How did the election of 2000 highlight both the weaknesses and strengths of America's election process?

The 2004 Presidential Campaign

THE CAMPAIGN BEGINS

As the 2004 presidential campaign began, four issues surfaced regarding the United States response to terrorism. First, in response to the September 11, 2001, attacks by al-Qaeda, the United States demanded that Afghanistan's Taliban government turn over al-Qaeda leader Osama bin Laden. When the Taliban refused, U.S. air strikes and ground forces drove the Taliban from power and weakened al-Qaeda's terrorist network.

Second, claiming that Iraq harbored weapons of mass destruction, the United States attacked Iraq. Following the fall of Baghdad and the capture of Saddam Hussein, the United States continued to maintain a military presence in Iraq. Americans were deeply divided. Some believed that the president was a strong and capable leader. Others believed that the war in Iraq was a huge mistake.

Third, at President Bush's urging, Congress passed the Patriot Act in response to the September 11 attacks. Designed to strengthen domestic security, the Patriot Act allowed law enforcement agencies greater freedom to investigate both citizens and non-citizens. A number of Americans, however, believed that the Patriot Act was contrary to the Constitution and the Bill of Rights because it undermined the right to privacy and other civil liberties.

Finally, the establishment of the U.S. Department of Homeland Security raised questions. This department issued directives requiring state and local governments to implement security measures. The cost of implementing the required measures caused a drain on state and local budgets, thereby further weakening an already sluggish economy.

The Candidates George W. Bush, a Republican, ran for a second term as president, while Senator John F. Kerry emerged as his Democratic challenger. While Bush had the advantage of being the incumbent, Kerry—having served four terms in the Senate—was also a seasoned politician.

In 2000, Bush had become president after an extremely close election. He lost the popular vote to his opponent, former Vice President Al Gore. However, after five weeks of recounts, the Electoral College declared Bush the winner. Bush had served two terms as Texas's governor.

In 2004, Vice President Richard Cheney was again Bush's running mate. Cheney served in the administrations of several Republican presidents, including President George H. W. Bush, father of the current president.

John Kerry of Massachusetts was first elected to the U.S. Senate in 1985. He was re-elected in 1990, 1996, and 2002. Kerry chose as his running mate John Edwards, one of Kerry's rivals in the Democratic primary. Edwards served one term as U.S. senator from North Carolina prior to running for the Democratic nomination. Before entering politics, both Kerry and Edwards practiced law.

The Primaries President Bush faced no serious opposition in the Republican primary. The Democratic primary, however, held plenty of drama. In addition to Kerry, seven other candidates initially entered the race: Carol Moseley Braun, Howard Dean, Richard Gephardt, Bob Graham, Dennis Kucinich, Joe Lieberman, and Al Sharpton. On May 3, 2003, the eight candidates met at the University of South Carolina to participate in the primary's first formal debate. Although they disagreed on most issues, the candidates all agreed that Bush's handling of the economy was poor.

In September, John Edwards and Wesley Clark, a retired general, joined the field as well. The field of candidates totaled ten. The field remained full until October 6, when Bob Graham became the first to drop out of the race.

The Internet played an active role in the campaign. In June, website MoveOn held the first online Democratic straw vote. Vermont Governor Howard Dean—an outspoken critic of President Bush—received 44 percent of more than 300,000 votes cast. Dennis Kucinich placed second, while John Kerry placed an unimpressive third with only 16 percent of the vote. Although the vote was not binding, it helped to strengthen Dean's position. Unlike other candidates, Dean's campaign heavily utilized the Internet to rally support, state his positions, and raise money. In December, Dean received an endorsement from former Vice President Al Gore. Dean also emerged as the Democratic front-runner in a CBS News /New York Times poll. However in January 2004, Dean slipped to third as John Kerry received the highest number of votes in the Iowa caucuses (contests that serve the same purpose as primary elections).

Kerry's victory in Iowa seemed to jumpstart his campaign. He continued to win in a significant number of primaries and caucuses. In February, Howard Dean ended his campaign. Less than a month later, Kerry had accumulated the number of delegates needed for nomination as the Democratic presidential candidate.

While Kerry was sewing up the Democratic nomination, consumer advocate Ralph Nader was making a bid for the Green Party's nomination. Although Nader had run as the Green Party candidate in 2000, the Greens nominated David Cobb, one of the founders of the Green Party of Texas. Months later, Nader announced that he would run as an independent, despite requests by Kerry and the Democratic National Committee that he not run. (Many Democrats believed that Nader, by running as an independent in the 2000 election, had caused Democratic candidate Al Gore to lose.) Nader said that he had decided to run again because "there's too much power and wealth in too few hands." Other third party candidates included Michael Badnarik, nominated by the United States Libertarian Party, and Constitution Party nominee Michael Peroutka.

BUSH VERSUS KERRY

With Kerry chosen as the Democratic nominee, the race for president focused on the two major candidates, Kerry and Bush. Both the Democratic and Republican campaigns used several strategies to reach and influence voters. First, they invested heavily in television and radio advertising. Second, the presidential candidates participated in three televised debates. Third, the candidates visited many locations throughout the United States to present their views and talk with voters. Most of the visits targeted swing states—states where the vote had been extremely close in the 2000 presidential election. They also launched all-out efforts to register new voters and get them to the polls.

The role of communications continued to expand. In addition to radio, television, and the print media, film and the Internet played important roles. Each campaign created a website where viewers could learn about the candidates, volunteer to work for the campaign, or donate money. Numerous movie theaters ran Michael Moore's controversial *Fahrenheit 9/11,* a film that severely criticized the Bush administration. The film *Going Upriver* documented Kerry's military experience in Vietnam. This prompted a group of Bush supporters, Swift Boat Veterans for Truth, to create ads discrediting Kerry's wartime record.

Issues, Counter-Issues, and Non-Issues Going into the election, Democrats identified the economy and the Iraq War as the main issues threatening Bush's re-election. The war was by far the most divisive. Before the war was launched, millions of people both in the United States and around the world protested the pending U.S. invasion of Iraq. The Bush administration claimed that Iraq was hiding weapons of mass destruction, and justified the invasion as necessary to the stamping out of terrorism. Opponents believed that the United States was rushing to war. They felt that the government should exhaust all other alternatives before committing troops to Iraq. Many also believed that the war was driven by U.S. desire for Mideast oil.

Even before invading troops failed to find weapons of mass destruction in Iraq, many concluded that Bush had not told the truth about the reason for the invasion. During the presidential debates, Kerry repeatedly claimed that President Bush had not been straightforward with the American people. Bush, on the other hand, maintained that the administration had received "flawed" intelligence regarding Iraq's weapons of mass destruction.

The Democratic Party believed that the economy would be a major campaign issue. The U.S. deficit was the largest ever, and continuing to grow. Dissatisfaction with the economy had risen from 13 percent of voters polled in 2000 to 52 percent polled in 2004. Bush's answer to the weak economy was permanent tax cuts. Kerry's plan

included "equal work for equal pay," a minimum wage that would increase with inflation, and no tax incentives for companies that outsource jobs to foreign countries.

To minimize the importance of these issues, the Bush campaign developed a strategy based on ideological conservatism. It stressed Bush's conservative ideas and attempted to show that they were very different from those of his opponent. Two of Bush's ideas revolved around the issues of abortion and gay marriages. Bush believed that both were morally wrong. Kerry stated that, as a Catholic, he was against abortion but that, if elected, he would not try to impose his moral and religious views on the American people. In defending his position, Kerry pointed to one of the principles on which the United States was founded, namely, the separation of church and state.

Regarding the gay marriage issue, Bush supported the proposed Federal Marriage Amendment, a constitutional amendment that would define marriage. Kerry opposed the amendment, stating that he believed in the protection of civil rights for all Americans, including gays and lesbians.

Other issues of concern to Americans included global warming and the state of the environment, the future of Social Security, and health care. However these issues played a minor role, if any, in the campaigns of either candidate.

Campaign Controversies During the campaign, several controversies arose. The first involved the military service of each candidate. In 1968, Bush enlisted in the Texas Air National Guard. At that time the United States was engaged in the Vietnam War but did not send members of the National Guard to fight in Vietnam. Instead, young men were drafted into military service. Hoping to avoid the draft, many attempted to enlist in the Guard. Filled to capacity, the National Guard created a waiting list for men hoping to join. Bush's critics contend that his family used its influence to gain his acceptance ahead of hundreds of others who were wait-listed. Some critics also claim that Bush received special consideration during his years in the Guard. Although many have sought information that would set the record straight, Bush's National Guard record remains controversial.

Unlike President Bush, Kerry served in Vietnam, where he was assigned to a swift boat—a fast coastal patrol boat. During his tour of duty, he was awarded three purple hearts, a silver star, and a bronze star. During the presidential campaign and more than thirty years later, a group calling itself Swift Boat Veterans for Truth (SBVT) raised questions about the appropriateness of Kerry's medals. However, only one SBVT member had served with Kerry on the same boat. A number of veterans who had served with Kerry came to his defense. In September 2004, the Navy Inspector General reviewed Kerry's combat medals. He determined that "the awards were properly approved."

Controversy also arose relative to the Bush campaign's creation of television ads using video footage of the September 11 terrorist attacks. Critics felt that the ads exploited personal tragedy for political gain. Bush's campaign spokespeople maintained that the ads were appropriate because the president's response to the attacks showed him at his best.

OHIO DETERMINES THE WINNER

Election Day On November 2 voter turnout was high. More than 120 million people—59 percent of eligible voters—cast ballots for president. Thousands of voters cast votes for the very first time. In many areas, people waited in line for hours. At some polling places, officials brought in extra voting machines to speed things up. At others, where lines were still long at closing time, officials kept polls open so that people could vote. The turnout reflected the fact that Americans were aware of the election process issues that occurred in the 2000 campaign. It also appeared that the election would be close—another reason for high voter turnout.

A Small Margin of Victory On the morning of November 3, neither candidate had the 270 electoral votes needed to win. Bush had 254 votes, two more than Kerry. Three states were still counting votes: Ohio, New Mexico, and Iowa. Since Iowa's 7 votes and New Mexico's 5 were not enough to elect either candidate, Ohio's 20 electoral votes were crucial. When Ohio's Secretary of State announced that the votes still to be counted were not enough to overtake Bush's slim lead of about 130,000, Kerry conceded. Bush received Iowa's and New Mexico's electoral votes as well as Ohio's.

The final totals were 286 electoral votes for Bush and 252 for Kerry. States on the West Coast and in the Northeast voted for Kerry, as did much of the Great Lakes region, while the South, Great Plains, and Rocky Mountain regions stood solidly behind Bush. The popular vote gave Bush only 2.46 percent more votes than Kerry—the smallest margin of victory ever received by a sitting U.S. president.

The Aftermath of the Election Following the election, groups such as Alliance for Democracy initiated recounts in Ohio and several other states. The recounts were mainly due to concerns over the reliability of electronic voting. Critics maintained that Direct Recording Electronic systems—voting machines not equipped to provide a paper trail—could be tampered with too easily. Although they recognized that the outcome of the election was not likely to change, supporters of the recounts viewed them as a tool for examining the accuracy and effectiveness of the election process.

On the day Electoral College votes were to be certified, a member of the House of Representatives and a Senator challenged the electoral votes of the state of Ohio. This was the second challenge to electoral votes since voting rules were established in 1877. The previous challenge was in 1969. The basis of the 2004 challenge rested on allegations of voter fraud. The challenge was rejected but was seen as a way to draw attention to the calls for national election reform.

As is common after a presidential election, Americans debated the continuing need for the Electoral College. Critics believe that the Electoral College is undemocratic because it does not necessarily reflect the popular vote. Instead, it is a system of winner take all on a state-by-state basis. Only Maine and Nebraska allow a split in their electoral votes according to the popular vote. Colorado voters cast ballots on an amendment that would allow the splitting of their electoral votes. The amendment failed, receiving only 34 percent of the vote. Critics further maintain that the system encourages candidates to campaign most heavily in states with the highest numbers of electoral votes. Thus states will few votes receive considerably less attention from the candidates.

With President Bush elected to a second term, Americans appeared more divided than ever. Traditionally, *Time* magazine selects the most influential person in the year's news. In December 2004, it named President Bush its "Person of the Year." Yet in a poll conducted by *Time,* less than half of adult Americans indicated that the president was doing a good job. Half of those surveyed also felt that the United States was "headed in the wrong direction."

Meanwhile, the president began building support for his plans to change the tax code structure and overhaul Social Security.

QUESTIONS

1. What political experience did George W. Bush and John F. Kerry have at the start of the 2004 presidential election?

2. Why was the Democratic primary of greater interest to voters than the Republican primary?

3. What were three key issues in the 2004 election, and what positions did the major candidates take on them?

4. In what way did the campaign focus on the personalities of the candidates? Do you think that personality should be an important factor in choosing a president? Explain.

5. What role did the Internet play in the campaign?

6. What controversies arose during the campaign? What influence, if any, do you think the controversies had on the voters? Explain.

7. There was much discussion of "moral issues" during the election of 2004. Do you think moral issues should be of concern in a presidential election? Why or why not?

8. What circumstances most likely explain the high voter turnout?

9. What concerns led to recounts in several states?

10. How did the election of 2004 highlight both the weaknesses and strengths of America's election process?

Electoral College Votes 1900–2004

This chart shows how the Electoral College has voted since 1900. The winning candidate must have a majority of the Electoral College votes to win. Electoral College votes were reallocated after the 2000 election.

| 3 | Democratic | / | Split Vote/Third Party | 3 | Republican | | Not Voting |

	McKinley (R)	T. Roosevelt (R)	Taft (R)	Wilson (D)	Wilson (D)	Harding (R)	Coolidge (R)	Hoover (R)	F. Roosevelt (D)	F. Roosevelt (D)	F. Roosevelt (D)	F. Roosevelt (D)	Truman (D)	Eisenhower (R)	Eisenhower (R)	Kennedy (D)	Johnson (D)	Nixon (R)	Nixon (R)	Carter (D)	Reagan (R)	Reagan (R)	G.H.W. Bush (R)	Clinton (D)	Clinton (D)	G.W. Bush (R)	G.W. Bush (R)
YEAR	00	04	08	12	16	20	24	28	32	36	40	44	48	52	56	60	64	68	72	76	80	84	88	92	96	00	04
AL	11	11	11	12	12	12	12	12	11	11	11	11	/	11	/	/	10	/	9	9	9	9	9	9	9	9	9
AK																3	3	3	3	3	3	3	3	3	3	3	3
AZ			3	3	3	3	3	3	3	3	4	4	4	4	4	5	5	6	6	6	6	7	7	8	8	8	10
AR	8	9	9	9	9	9	9	9	9	9	9	9	9	8	8	8	6	/	6	6	6	6	6	6	6	6	6
CA	9	10	10	/	13	13	13	13	22	22	22	25	25	32	32	32	40	40	45	45	45	47	47	54	54	54	55
CO	4	5	5	6	6	6	6	6	6	6	6	6	6	6	6	6	6	7	7	7	7	8	8	8	8	8	9
CT	6	7	7	7	7	7	7	7	8	8	8	8	8	8	8	8	8	8	8	8	8	8	8	8	8	8	7
DE	3	3	3	3	3	3	3	3	3	3	3	3	3	3	3	3	3	3	3	3	3	3	3	3	3	3	3
DC																3	3	3	3	3	3	3	3	3	3	3	3
FL	4	5	5	6	6	6	6	6	7	7	7	8	8	10	10	10	14	14	17	17	17	21	21	25	25	25	27
GA	13	13	13	14	14	14	14	14	12	12	12	12	12	12	12	12	12	/	12	12	12	12	12	13	13	13	15
HI																3	4	4	4	4	4	4	4	4	4	4	4
ID	3	3	3	4	4	4	4	4	4	4	4	4	4	4	4	4	4	4	4	4	4	4	4	4	4	4	4
IL	24	27	27	29	29	29	29	29	29	29	29	28	28	27	27	27	26	26	26	26	26	24	24	22	22	22	21
IN	15	15	15	15	15	15	15	15	14	14	14	13	13	13	13	13	13	13	13	13	13	12	12	12	12	12	11
IA	13	13	13	13	13	13	13	13	11	11	11	10	10	10	10	10	9	9	8	8	8	8	8	7	7	7	7
KS	10	10	10	10	10	10	10	10	9	9	9	8	8	8	8	8	7	7	7	7	7	7	6	6	6	6	6
KY	13	13	13	13	13	13	13	13	11	11	11	11	11	10	10	10	10	9	9	9	9	9	9	8	8	8	8
LA	8	9	9	10	10	10	10	10	10	10	10	10	/	10	10	10	10	/	10	10	10	10	10	9	9	9	9
ME	6	6	6	6	6	6	6	6	5	5	5	5	5	5	5	5	4	4	4	4	4	4	4	4	4	4	4
MD	8	/	/	8	8	8	8	8	8	8	8	8	8	9	9	9	10	10	10	10	10	10	10	10	10	10	10
MA	15	16	16	18	18	18	18	18	17	17	17	16	16	16	16	16	14	14	14	14	14	13	13	12	12	12	12
MI	14	14	14	15	15	15	15	15	19	19	19	19	19	20	20	20	21	21	21	21	21	20	20	18	18	18	17
MN	9	11	11	12	12	12	12	12	11	11	11	11	11	11	11	11	10	10	10	10	10	10	10	10	10	10	10
MS	9	10	10	10	10	10	10	10	9	9	9	9	/	8	8	8	7	/	7	7	7	7	7	7	7	7	6
MO	17	18	18	18	18	18	18	18	15	15	15	15	15	13	13	13	12	12	12	12	12	11	11	11	11	11	11
MT	3	3	3	4	4	4	4	4	4	4	4	4	4	4	4	4	4	4	4	4	4	4	4	3	3	3	3
NE	8	8	8	8	8	8	8	8	7	7	7	6	6	6	6	6	5	5	5	5	5	5	5	5	5	5	5
NV	3	3	3	3	3	3	3	3	3	3	3	3	3	3	3	3	3	3	3	3	3	4	4	4	4	4	5
NH	4	4	4	4	4	4	4	4	4	4	4	4	4	4	4	4	4	4	4	4	4	4	4	4	4	4	4
NJ	10	12	12	14	14	14	14	14	16	16	16	16	16	16	16	16	17	17	17	17	17	16	16	15	15	15	15
NM			3	3	3	3	3	3	3	3	4	4	4	4	4	4	4	4	4	4	4	5	5	5	5	5	5
NY	36	39	39	45	45	45	45	45	47	47	47	47	47	45	45	45	43	43	41	41	41	36	36	33	33	33	31
NC	11	12	12	12	12	12	12	12	13	13	13	14	14	14	14	14	13	/	13	13	13	13	13	14	14	14	15
ND	3	4	4	5	5	5	5	5	4	4	4	4	4	4	4	4	4	4	3	3	3	3	3	3	3	3	3
OH	23	23	23	24	24	24	24	24	26	26	26	25	25	25	25	25	26	26	25	25	25	23	23	21	21	21	20
OK			7	10	10	10	10	10	11	11	11	10	10	8	8	/	8	8	8	8	8	8	8	8	8	8	7
OR	4	4	4	5	5	5	5	5	5	5	5	6	6	6	6	6	6	6	6	6	6	7	7	7	7	7	8
PA	32	34	34	/	38	38	38	38	36	36	36	35	35	32	32	32	29	29	27	27	27	25	25	23	23	23	21
RI	4	4	4	5	5	5	5	5	4	4	4	4	4	4	4	4	4	4	4	4	4	4	4	4	4	4	4
SC	9	9	9	9	9	9	9	9	8	8	8	8	/	8	8	8	8	8	8	8	8	8	8	8	8	8	8
SD	4	4	4	/	5	5	5	4	4	4	4	4	4	4	4	4	4	4	4	4	4	3	3	3	3	3	3
TN	12	12	12	12	12	12	12	12	11	11	11	12	/	11	11	11	11	11	10	10	10	11	11	11	11	11	11
TX	15	18	18	20	20	20	20	20	23	23	23	23	23	24	24	24	25	25	26	26	26	29	29	32	32	32	34
UT	3	3	3	4	4	4	4	4	4	4	4	4	4	4	4	4	4	4	4	4	4	5	5	5	5	5	5
VT	4	4	4	4	4	4	4	4	3	3	3	3	3	3	3	3	3	3	3	3	3	3	3		3	3	3
VA	12	12	12	12	12	12	12	12	11	11	11	11	11	12	12	12	12	12	/	12	12	12	12	13	13	13	13
WA	4	5	5	/	7	7	7	7	8	8	8	8	8	9	9	9	9	9	9	9	/	9	10	10	11	11	11
WV	6	7	7	8	/	8	8	8	8	8	8	8	8	8	8	8	7	7	6	6	6	6	6	5	5	5	5
WI	12	13	13	13	13	13	/	13	12	12	12	12	12	12	12	12	12	12	11	11	11	11	11	11	11	11	10
WY	3	3	3	3	3	3	3	3	3	3	3	3	3	3	3	3	3	3	3	3	3	3	3	3	3	3	3
Total Vote	447	476	483	531	531	531	531	531	531	531	531	531	531	531	531	537	538	538	538	538	538	538	538	538	538	538	538
Total Winner	292	336	321	435	277	404	382	444	472	523	449	432	303	442	457	303	486	301	520	297	489	525	426	370	379	271	274

Compare and Contrast Elections, 1900—2004

Select two elections and use the information in this Handbook to answer the following

COMPARE AND CONTRAST

1. Identify the presidential candidates by name, party, and election year.

_____

2. Contrast the candidates' views on economic policy.

_____

_____

3. Describe the relationship of popular vote (p. 2–3) to the electoral vote.

_____

_____

_____

EXPLAINING HISTORICAL PATTERNS

1. What is the voting pattern in your state?

_____

_____

2. How is your state's record alike or different from its neighboring states?

_____

_____

_____

3. What patterns for the Republican and Democratic parties surround the two election years selected?

_____

_____

_____

How to Conduct a Mock Election

Mock Election simulations take time to organize and execute but can make a lasting impression on students. Some or all of the following suggestions can be used to conduct a campaign and election.

STEP I: ORGANIZE POLITICAL PARTIES

A. Survey student opinion about specific issues to determine orientation toward Republican or Democratic parties.

B. Place on chalkboard or distribute copies of survey questions, such as:

Do you support...	Yes	No
1. a subminimum wage for teenagers?	_____	_____
2. a national drinking age?	_____	_____
3. a national draft?	_____	_____
4. school search of student lockers for reasonable cause?	_____	_____
5. cuts in federal student loans to help balance the budget?	_____	_____
6. strong gun control?	_____	_____
7. affirmative action programs?	_____	_____
8. capital punishment?	_____	_____
9. increased personal income taxes?	_____	_____
10. increased corporate income taxes?	_____	_____
11. increased defense spending?	_____	_____
12. reduced social services spending?	_____	_____
13. reduced foreign imports?	_____	_____
14. subsidies on agricultural production?	_____	_____
15. protective tariffs?	_____	_____
16. sanctions against Iraq?	_____	_____

C. Count the number of **yes** and **no** responses to opinion questions. If you use those above, students with seven or more **yes** responses would tend to be Republican. Give these students a red sticker (or other symbol) to designate them as members of the Republican party. Using the above questions, students with seven or more **no** responses would tend to be Democratic. Give these students a blue sticker (or other symbol) for their designation in the Democratic party.

STEP II: ORGANIZE PARTY CONVENTIONS TO NOMINATE CANDIDATES

A. Ask each party to select two or more candidates to run for President. Candidates can volunteer to be drafted by the party or can be assigned by the teacher.

B. Candidates must prepare and give a five-minute speech to identify their stands on the issues and to persuade their party to nominate them to run for President.

C. Each national convention nominates its candidate by roll call vote. A winner is declared when one candidate receives over 50 percent of the party vote. If no candidate receives 50 percent on the first ballot, additional speeches, roll calls, or special caucuses may take place. Roll calls for each national convention can be done simultaneously or consecutively.

STEP III: ORGANIZE A CAMPAIGN STRATEGY

A. Each political party should select a Vice-Presidential running mate and a campaign manager.

B. To formulate a campaign strategy, have the President, Vice-President, and campaign manager for both parties determine where and how they will campaign after considering the following questions:

    1. Which five states are most important to your campaign?

    2. What three issues will you emphasize in your campaign?

    3. How do you rank the effectiveness of television, radio, print advertising, and personal appearances?

    4. How will you allocate your resources of time, money, and people in this campaign?

C. The campaign team should decide which states represented by students should receive the greatest emphasis and campaign materials.

D. Assign each student to represent a specific number of votes in a specific state by dividing the voting population of that state (use 100,000,000 voters) by the number of students assigned to the state.

E. Each political party and/or campaign team should prepare a thirty-second television or radio advertisement for its candidate.

F. Others could create a political cartoon or write a newspaper ad or editorial to support their candidates or attack the opponents.

STEP IV: ORGANIZE A POLITICAL DEBATE OR PRESS CONFERENCE

A. Candidates should prepare brief statements identifying their views on foreign, economic, and social issues.

B. Other students should prepare questions about foreign, economic, and social issues to ask either candidate.

C. Sponsor a debate or press conference between Presidential candidates. Candidates could begin or conclude the debate with the position statements they have prepared. Students could question the candidates. Questions and responses should be timed.

D. After the debate, or press conference, students should evaluate the performance of each candidate and write an editorial endorsement of their preferred candidate.

STEP V: ORGANIZE A POPULAR ELECTION

A. Designate a panel of four election judges who have the responsibility of voter registration and vote tallying.

B. Give the class a limited time (one day to one week) to register with an election judge to vote. Voter registration should include a specified state designation.

C. On election day, the election judges distribute ballots to each registered voter. Voters should cast secret ballots.

D. Election judges count the votes and announce the results of the popular vote.

E. The winning candidate delivers an acceptance speech; the loser gives a concession speech.

ANSWERS

2000 Campaign

1. A number of Americans had grown weary of Clinton, and Republicans believed that voters wanted a change in Washington.

2. Similarities: Both men came from political families. Differences: Gore had more political experience, while Bush was a businessman who entered politics much later.

3. A member of Congress would be more familiar with the political system in Washington and thus would know how to get legislation passed. An outsider might bring fresh ideas to the presidency and have a better grasp on the problems and concerns of Americans living beyond the capital.

4. Advantage: forces candidates to sharpen their campaign skills and establish a focused message. Disadvantage: forces candidates to spend precious financial resources.

5. Taxes—Bush proposed a $1.3 trillion cut in tax rates; Gore offered a smaller tax cut. Social Security—Bush proposed allowing workers to invest some of their Social Security taxes in the stock market; Gore proposed using interest savings from reducing the debt to shore up Social Security. Health care—Bush proposed a $2,000 tax credit for families to buy insurance; Gore proposed providing every child with insurance and expanding coverage for poor and middle-class families.

6. The networks predicted Florida for Gore and then took back that prediction. Later, they declared the state for Bush and thus declared him the next president. However, they had to take back that prediction a short time later.

7. With a near even split in Congress, Democrats and Republicans would have to face the difficult task of trying to win over members of the opposing party in order to get legislation passed.

8. Some students will say yes because the system forces candidates to campaign in many close states. Others may say no because it undermines majority rule.

9. Some students may say it is important for a president to set a strong moral example for the country. Others may say that it is more important for a president to focus on achieving important domestic and foreign policy goals.

10. Weaknesses—showed that the country's voting system is prone to error. Strengths—showed that the United States is a nation that obeys its laws, and that no matter how divisive the race may be, the transfer of power is always peaceful.

2004 Campaign

1. George Bush was the incumbent president and previously served two terms as Governor of Texas. John Kerry served four terms in the United States Senate.

2. The Democratic primary featured ten candidates whose political views spanned a wide variety of views.

3. Three issues included the war in Iraq, the economy, and moral issues. Bush supported the war as a means to eliminate terrorism, offered tax cuts to spur the economy, and was against abortion rights and gay marriage. Kerry believed Bush entered the war before all avenues had been exhausted, was opposed to tax cuts, supported a minimum wage, and was supportive of abortion rights and civil liberties including gays and lesbians.

4. The war records of each man were questioned. Answers will vary but should include an explanation of the student's position.

5. The Internet provided web sites with information on candidates' positions, fund raising for the campaign, and offered opportunities for volunteer work on the campaigns.

6. Controversies included the question of the Iraq war and the alleged weapons of mass destruction, and the war records of each candidate.

7. Answers will vary but should include an explanation of the student's position.

8. High election turnout can be attributed to voter interest; voter concern over election process, newly registered voters, and the tightness of the race.

9. Questions over election processes and concerns about the reliability of electronic voting.

10. High interest in the campaign brought out many voters and included many new voters, which is an indication of a widening democratic process. The controversies about the issues divided many voters and created a division between voters throughout the country.

Notes